App Trillionaires

App Trillionaires:
How To Become An App Developer

Enjoy <u>Life</u>, Make <u>Money</u>, and
Live Your <u>Dreams</u>!

ABHINAV GUPTA

iUniverse, Inc.
Bloomington

APP TRILLIONAIRES: HOW TO BECOME AN APP DEVELOPER
ENJOY LIFE, MAKE MONEY, AND LIVE YOUR DREAMS!

iUniverse books may be ordered through booksellers or by contacting:

iUniverse
1663 Liberty Drive
Bloomington, IN 47403
www.iuniverse.com
1-800-Authors (1-800-288-4677)

Library of Congress Control Number: 2013900222

ISBN: 978-1-4759-7043-2 (sc)
ISBN: 978-1-4759-7041-8 (hc)
ISBN: 978-1-4759-7042-5 (e)

Printed in the United States of America

iUniverse rev. date: 1/9/2013

RAVE REVIEWS FOR APP TRILLIONAIRES!

"This book contains a plethora of practical tips and gives a great overview of the apps business. But its essence is really the philosophical approach that is something way more important than technical tricks. For that reason, I highly recommend this book for everyone that would want to take the apps business train, including experienced developers."

Nicolas Peri, CTO of Stonetrip (http://www.stonetrip.com)

"Abhinav uses his real world experiences in breaking into the App development business to great effect in this book. For those just getting into the field, you'll find dozens of pearls of wisdom, with tips and pointers on all that you need to get started making and marketing great mobile Apps."

Russell Hansen, Synaptic Bytes (http://synapticbytes.com)

"Abhinav Gupta has created a truly amazing collection of development tips, insights and advice summarized into an easy to read book. Even I myself, a long time professional, found some new ideas to try while reading this well organized journey into the world of mobile app development."

Attila Beke, 3D Magic LLC

DEDICATION

Being an App Developer and App Business Owner is a challenge and there are many times when everyone will not understand you or may not understand HOW you are able to do what you do. Out of frustration, anger, jealousy, envy and even greed, many will try and reduce your dreams or belittle you either because they themselves have given up on their own dreams, or they have not taken the risks to achieve success in their own lives. In any case, keeping a positive mindset and having a strong faith in a greater power is key to success in this business.

For this reason, first and foremost, this book is dedicated to God who has helped me through some of the toughest times in my life when the whole world was against me and said I was crazy to believe that I could achieve success. I'd also like to thank my wife Seema and my kids and family who have stuck by my side through the good times and the bad times. I'd also like to thank my team around the world who helped me out in building this business, especially Amit Niraj who also kept a positive and loyal mindset when things just seemed down.

And to my valued readers and supporters, thank you all from the bottom of my heart for your constant support and interest in the creations I have made. I pray and hope you will continue to purchase and enjoy the many works I create.

Abhinav Gupta
Lead Developer and CEO
Game Scorpion Inc.
http://www.gamescorpion.com

TABLE OF CONTENTS

"The starting point of all achievement is DESIRE. Keep this constantly in mind. Weak desires bring weak results, just as a small amount of fire makes a small amount of heat."

— *Napoleon Hill, Think and Grow Rich*

1. WHO AM I?

My name is Abhinav Gupta, a person who was born and raised in Ontario, Canada. My ancestry is of South East Asian (Indian) decent, and even though I can speak the Indian languages fluently, I have only visited India 2-3 times in my life. Canada has and always will be my home, but knowing how I got here is also very important as well, and for this reason I celebrate my ancestral culture as well as my Canadian roots. One of the best things that I love about Canada is the fact that I can walk down the street and say hello to people in their own languages. It's the way the world should be in my opinion, a place where all human beings work together and celebrate their differences and love each other and respect each other.

I'm an App Developer, App Business Owner/Trainer, a Father to two beautiful children, married to a wonderful wife with a cute little Maltese dog and a very strong believer in God and the Bible. I'm a graduate of Computer Science from Ryerson University in Toronto, Ontario, Canada and I've been in the IT field for well over 10 years.

Since I was a young boy, making and playing video games was always a love of mine and since then I wanted to learn how I could do that for the rest of my life. I have always loved to create things and so creativity and innovation have been a driving force for me.

You may have been wondering WHY I decided to write this book. If I know how to make money and can show others how to make money, wouldn't I want to just hide the secret and keep it all to myself?

It started back in 2008 when the recession hit me here in Canada. I personally believe that it was due to this VERY mentality of GREED. American Corporate and personal greed hit an all time high! Banks were giving out mortgages to people who didn't even qualify for a mortgage, just to try and make even more money. PUBLIC COMPANIES had CEO's making MILLIONS UPON MILLIONS of dollars while their staff barely could make ends meet! The American market collapsed and the whole world went into a recession!

You may ask why I'm bringing this all up...Well that's when I lost my computer contract (I was working at the time fixing computers). At that point I owned a house, a car and had a young family (Wife, son and dog) and did not know what to do. I started applying for jobs, and here I was with a Degree in Computer Science (Graduated from Ryerson University in that year) and I could not find a job. To try and keep afloat I opened up a Dollar Store and Computer Store in Brampton, Ontario with whatever little nest egg I had left, and also found work selling a glorified Lint Roller in various Department Stores in Ontario. As the recession had just started and was getting worse, sales in the two businesses were just horrid, and my other side job selling the Lint Rollers was not paying off anything...And then at the end of 2008 what I did not think was possible actually happened to me...like many people in North America and the world...I went bankrupt.

I begged my parents to move in, it was a very low time in my life, but I kept faith in the higher power and kept believing that God had a plan and I knew I was going to be in a better place. At the time however I did not know what to do and I was a bit depressed. Loosing everything you have is not a great feeling at all.

Time and time again I would look at the news only to see more doom and gloom and many corporations that you thought were "too big to fail" going bankrupt and dying out! Some of the top banks were just wrapping up and leaving thousands without money! It was a frenzy, people were not sure whether to even trust BANKS! Do you keep your money under a bed now? Like these were at that time SERIOUS QUESTIONS!

I put my resume out to many places in North America (Both Canada and the US) only to get 2 interviews which were not fruitful at all.

I took whatever little I had left and started doing computer repair and opened up a side business in computer repair after that. It started to grow and was helping me to pay the bills. Then at the end of 2010 this little world of apps was shown to me. Steve Jobs had brought out the next iPhone and was promoting apps and this world of micro-software products that were starting to "REVOLUTIONIZE" the way we all lived and worked.

I thought hey lets check it out…And I was hooked! Since I was 10 years old I always aimed at being a video game developer and this was the perfect opportunity. It seemed like a higher power was at work even though I did not understand it, but due to personal reasons, I had to close up my Computer Repair business. I took whatever I had earned and saved up for a while and went full force into the App world and Thank God, since then, I have been moving forward and growing daily!

Now today I'm the CEO of a successful app business with over 25+ apps in over 10+ marketplaces and growing even more! I look back at those days of the Recession and Greed at the cost of others, and I truly believe that we can make a better world by having more RESPONSIBLE MILLIONAIRES rather than GREEDY people.

This is why I decided to write this book. I want to help people who share the same vision of not only helping themselves and their families, but to also give back to their local communities.

That is my mission with this book. If you follow what I have outlined here; follow my programs and use my tools and resources I am continuously creating and bringing out; you should most likely (no guarantees here, you get out what you put into it!) become quite wealthy financially. However keeping it all to yourself would just repeat a history that I do not wish on ANYONE!

This is MY goal here to help build or create RESPONSIBLE successful people who are charitable and believe in a higher power, not just plain greedy. You can't take your money with you when you die.

So now you know who I am and why I have decided to create this book. But WHY ARE YOU HERE? Have you figured out WHY you are doing this?

"Many dream a dream and wake up to reality…some dream a dream and MAKE IT A REALITY!"

— Abhinav Gupta, 2008

2. IS THIS BOOK FOR YOU?

This book deals with technology and is geared towards those who like technology, and dare I say it, LOVE Technology! You may have heard from people who claim that you do not need to know programming nor even like computers to run an app business. Sure you can run this business without even touching a computer; however it is a very unrealistic approach to the Mobile App Business.

By reading this book you are looking at the possibility of starting a Mobile SOFTWARE Application Business that CREATES Mobile Applications. I can assure you, you require technology and a love for creating things. Programming will DEFINITLY come up along your path in this business!

If you hate technology and hate programming, well I won't lie to you or lead you on. My full recommendation at this point if you fall into that category is to stop reading now and do yourself a favor and go find another business or profession. By you starting an app business with no love for technology or computers, you'd be better off taking your nest egg to Las Vegas or your local casino and you'd probably have a better chance of success there. That's not to say that you can't do it, you definitely can achieve anything you believe you can, but you'd have to develop a total love for technology and programming in order to make this business a true success.

I've seen too many people start this business with wrong impressions thinking that it's really EASY MONEY or that it's a business that they can outsource everything and put things on "Auto-Pilot"…HA!

No business can start without you actually taking steps towards running it and making it work. As I said earlier you get out of it what you put into it! YES there arc special tools and methods that may make this business a bit easier or faster to run or get closer to "Auto-Pilot", but you HAVE to do work to get them setup properly! You have to make the calls, you have to setup the accounts, you have to get the apps created, you have to keep your business up to date, you have to outsource and build the right team, etc.

Can you do this part time? SURE!

Can you do it full time? MOST DEFINITELY!

But can you do this on Auto-Pilot? Let me just suffice it to say that I have been in this business for several years now, and I can assure you there is no magic Auto-Pilot button out there, even though there are some tools and systems that help you to get CLOSE. This is a **business** at the end of the day and the faster you can get out of your head that this is some sort of Get-Rich-Quick scheme, the faster you'll be on your way to true success.

Let me tell you something, you CAN make money while you sleep in this business, but it takes months if not years to setup correctly. It's not something that just happens overnight. In fact if you research those who are overnight success stories, the interesting thing you may find is that those so called overnight success stories took years in the making. No success comes without a solid amount of work and dedication and persistence behind it backed by solid Faith and Belief!

Auto-Pilot is just not realistic in my opinion because you still need to take part in your business and not knowing technology or any programming at all when you're running a SOFTWARE BUSINESS is definitely a whole load of nonsense!

How many **SUCCESSFUL** Real Estate agents do you know who know nothing about houses? How about **SUCCESSFUL** car salesmen who know nothing about a car? So how far do you think you'll go in your new found App Business without knowing anything about Technology and SOFTWARE **APP**lications?

So if you are reading this thinking that you are going to make a quick buck and won't have to lift a finger to do any work at all, then I've got news for you...THIS IS NOT A GET-RICH-QUICK-SCHEME! Get-Rich-Quick is something I like to call *Get-Poor-Fast!*

"Be not afraid of greatness: some are born great, some achieve greatness, and some have greatness thrust upon them."

— **William Shakespeare**

3. THE APP BUSINESS

Today more than ever more people are purchasing mobile phones and tablets. The growth is so explosive that an entire industry has been created around mobile software applications, known as "APPS".

The App Business is one of the hottest businesses to get into and is expected to grow even faster this year in 2013 and beyond! Many have started such businesses with investments as small as 10k-15k US Dollars and have become very wealthy!

In fact in many cases, the wealth has been so explosive that people have been quitting their day jobs and turning to app development and the app business full time.

This business has helped people spend more time with their families, traveling the world and living their dreams. In fact, as you are reading this book right now, I'm making money! That's the beauty of this business; you make money while you sleep *LITERALLY*!

However don't confuse this with a get rich quick scheme, it is not. It takes years to get to this level, and a lot of dedication. I've seen many people start in this business only to fail due to having a wrong mentality of the business and what it's all about. This is not a magical business that will make you a millionaire overnight, even though there have been several cases in the past where this has happened.

Let me be realistic with you, firstly, it takes MANY apps realistically to make money in this industry. If you research Rovio, the company behind the popular app Angry Birds, you will learn that they themselves had built something like 50 apps before hitting massive success with Angry Birds. I'm not here to give you all kinds of fake hype and tell you that I have some magic pill to make you rich. What I do have is

TRIED AND TESTED METHODS that I have used successfully to build an app business with over 25+ apps in many markets that allows me to live the life most people dream about.

So that is the goal here, to get you to a point where you can realistically make this into a business that can help you to some day quit your day job and start living the life you always wanted. I pray and hope that you'll be able to use your new found money to not only help yourself and your loved ones but also to help out your own local communities.

If the knowledge I share in this book can help in making abundant successful people who love what they do, it is my hope that through these pages I can also build responsible "rich people". I lost nearly everything I had to the recession in 2008 and I can attribute that in my honest opinion, to irresponsible "rich people". The corporations who were greedy for money, who were too concerned about their own pockets than to make sure their employees who filled those very pockets had a roof over their head and food on their plate.

However, I'm grateful to God that I did end up going through that because I would have never started this business if I had not lost nearly everything, and this book would have never been written. I would not wish that fate of near Bankruptcy, loosing your house, car and nearly your family all due to the greed of others on anyone! So I do plead with you as a reader, that WHEN you make it in this business, and I'm assuming that you are in this to be successful, make sure that you are responsible with your new found riches.

Being "rich" is not just abundance in money, but it's the quality of life that one lives. Having great faith, loving and helping out others, having wonderful health, love and appreciation from your family and peers, being able to enjoy your life to the fullest on your terms, and every day being able to *SMILE*! Those things that money can't buy are in my opinion true "richness" and if you have those bases covered, then financial riches will just magnify those qualities even more.

Let us first start off with a quick exercise I like to call the *SMILE* exercise. That's right, go ahead and give yourself the biggest smile from ear to ear! It should be so wide that your cheeks start to hurt a bit! Hold that for about 10 seconds and repeat 3 times. This should put you into a state of mind that goes hand in hand with success, a positive *CAN DO* mindset! If you start reading this book with that mentality every time you pick it up, you'll have a better chance at success than others do at this business.

You may be wondering why such trivial things are so important to this business and may think that I may have lost my mind! I can assure you that this business is full of ups and downs and a LOT of negativity. People rarely get the chance to live a life of dreams where they can travel as they want, spend time with their families and be their own boss.

There will be jealous people, envious people, hateful people and many others who will just try and put down this new business venture idea from the beginning! Let me be real with you, any business you start will require some risks to be taken. I can assure you that in this business, the rewards are definitely worth it if you put your effort and time into it.

Lets just go over some of the many reasons why this business is the ULTIMATE business that everyone is trying to get into now more than ever before.

Reason #1: Multiple Markets to Make Money

The Apple App Store is one of the largest App Stores in the world and is also the original home of what are now commonly known as Apps. Along with the Apple App Store there are many other market places in which Apps are currently being sold. One of the most known ones is Android Google Play Market which is owned by Google.

Reason #2: New and Fresh Market

Apps have been compared many times to the website industry when it just started, in which websites were sought after by business owners and companies. Mobile Apps are now going through the same fate as many new business owners are looking to find people to develop apps for their respective businesses. Not only do Mobile Apps share that in common with the website world, another emerging and important area that is now starting to really form is that of ASO or App Store Optimization.

In the website world we call this SEO or Search Engine Optimization. I will be going over some basics of ASO throughout this book however the goal of this book is to get you started in creating a successful app business using a step-by-step method. I believe the step-by-step method is the best way and will help you avoid many of the common pitfalls and mistakes that myself and many other new App Business Owners have faced when just starting this business.

Reason #3: Apps are GROWING!

2013 will introduce new and emerging areas in which apps will be used. From OUYA which is a brand new video game console based on Android, to kitchen appliances and automobiles with apps built into them. Imagine being able to put a beer into the fridge only to have your phone alert you when it's ready to drink! Or imagine being able to set the laundry wash/rinse cycle while riding on the train to work! This will start to become the reality over the next years as mobile app technology will start becoming a part of everything we do. This industry is definitely growing and is planned to keep growing at an exponential rate!

Reason #4: New Products, App Stores and Opportunities for Profit

From Microsoft to Amazon, there are many companies bringing out new devices and various app stores and products to sell apps in. This presents an opportunity to take an app you make and place it on sale on various app markets around the world, thus increasing your chance at profits.

Reason #5: The Freedom

This is a great benefit of running a mobile app business. You get the freedom of being a business owner, and that too a MOBILE one! You can pick up and travel at any time and still run your business full force from anywhere in the world that an Internet Connection exists! I personally started this business because I was visiting another Country and was not able to manage my struggling IT Business at the time. I had customers who expected me to physically be there and I couldn't. This in turn made me loose contracts and relationships which was quite painful. A mobile app business will allow you to be anywhere in the world and still run the business without issues. It truly is a dream business in my opinion!

Reason #6: The Money

Notice I put this reason for getting into the App Business last? Everyone always tries to hype this up, that you'll get rich overnight. Yes you WILL make money in this business, even while sleeping, but I want you to understand that the money is just a by-product of running this business. That aside, you WILL see money coming in, even while you sleep! This business is really great in the fact that the more apps you make, the more money you make. You can literally hand out apps for free and STILL make money via in-app advertisements and in-app purchases! The money is great and I've seen many who make thousands every week if not every day! It doesn't happen overnight however and will take you at least a year or two in my opinion to see a solid return on your investment. Keep in mind however that results will vary so don't expect that you will get that. You could very well make less than that, or quite possibly even more, and it all depends on your efforts.

HOW MUCH MONEY CAN YOU MAKE SERIOUSLY?

Wow is that EVER the million dollar question there! I get asked this all the time! Let me give you a few tips on this, because many of you are going to start off with some pre-conceived negative and dare I say it, outrageous claims that you have probably heard from other people.

Firstly I've heard most if not all these claims, from, "My friend from out of town develops apps and is a millionaire and drives this nice car, etc." to the age old, "The guy made 6 figures in a weekend making a stupid little fart app!"

Making apps firstly is a challenge! Making money from apps consistently and successfully is another challenge. That being said let me tell you my experience and what you will most likely see as a reality when getting into the app world. Now before I begin, let me point out that those stories that you hear may very well be TRUE and I don't doubt that they are. However understand that if they are true, those same stories are what I like to call OUTLINERS in this business. They are not the REALITY in this business for most developers in general.

Can you make millions overnight? YES! However that's like saying you also have the potential of becoming a millionaire tomorrow by purchasing a lottery ticket. Now tell me, if you purchase a lottery ticket, can you also make millions overnight? Of course you can, that is if you hit the correct numbers. The odds of you hitting those numbers are quite large! The same holds true for the app world!

When things were just starting out in the app world, there were a handful of apps and a handful of developers. Fast forward now many years later and we have nearly a million apps in the Apple App Store and hundreds of thousands of developers worldwide and millions more on the way! Everyone is trying to get into the app world and the competition is fierce! If you think that you are going to make it with just one app… well let me enlighten you on the same mistake I went through and a common mistake that most app developers fall into.

The Angry Bird Trap

When I first started working on my first app I thought I had the next big hit! I thought I was going to be the next big Angry Birds! This is a common idea that brand new developers start off with. They see some big app out there or come up with some big app idea they believe is worth millions and then invest every last cent into it.

My first app was Melina's Conquest, a very ambitious 3D Retro Role Playing Game! By any standards, that game was quite technical and had thousands upon thousands of lines of code. I spent 8 months on it with a few developers and volunteers and I personally was working daily for 8 months around 12-15 hours EVERY DAY non-stop to try and get the game finished. I invested thousands into this endeavor thinking that I was working on the next big hit! 20+ levels in full Retro style 3D!

In fact there was one point where I spent 2-3 weeks with less than a few hours of sleep per day and massive amounts of energy drinks and coffee.

Not only did I nearly die from this (I was drinking 2-3+ energy drinks daily, with a few coffees, power bars, and literally very little sleep and only McDonalds as my food source!) I also burnt out and was on my very last amounts of money!

The moment of truth came when I finally released the app and spent a few thousand on marketing as well. From Press releases to free app download websites to contests and much more, I had done every single thing by the book and beyond the book!

The game launched and in my first month…(DRUMROLL PLEASE)…I brought in a total of…LESS THAN $200 US DOLLARS! (In retrospect, I placed my app at $4.99 and had no LITE/FREE version, nor did I have any form of advertising or other forms of monetization built in. No push notifications, no extra special things, no game center, nothing but a plain app at just $4.99. This was doomed from the beginning!)

Shattered, confused, dazed, sad, bitter, and nearly giving up on life, lets just suffice it to say I was in tears nearly, screaming loud at the top of my lungs while driving a van that I didn't even want in the first place, and everything around me just SUCKED!

This is the turning point in my story, and the ultimate reason why I told you earlier that faith and a major reason why you're doing this are going to be important to you when running this business. You will have those times where things just don't make sense and you've invested thousands in an app and a lot of time only to yield horrible results!

I started immediately to stop blaming God and started to become REALLY GREATFUL for all the things in life I DID have, like a roof over my head, food on my plate, I was alive with a beautiful wife and kids that love me and were with me through the tough times. At this point I reflected on why I got into this in the first place; because I had a true love for making video games and apps. I knew that this was my calling and I would do everything I could to master it. I knew this is what I wanted to do in my life, I wanted to be successful at it and make a real living from it and enjoy my life from the fruits that come from creating things.

At that moment I had an epiphany…"Just take one more step…make another app, really fast, without spending 8 months. You've learned how to make apps over the past 8 months. Now replicate what you have done and try and make a single app in 1 month or less!"

Hmmm what a thought! If I could reduce the time it took to make an app and start making an app in 1 month or less, I could potentially DOUBLE UP what I was bringing in. It wasn't going to bring back the thousands of dollars I lost, but it would at least start giving me hope that one day this business could potentially lead me to a very lucrative future.

That's when I was able to build Intimate Fireplace with the help of my friend and colleague Amit. We also built ASRI Astral Space Racer Infinity which was another 3D Space racing game.

Those two apps took me about 1.5 months to create right after Melina's Conquest and with very little out of my pocket because I now had all the tools and experience I needed to make apps that I could just replicate what I did and reuse code from Melina's Conquest.

With 3 apps in the Apple App Store, I started looking to alternative markets to try and get into and start making money. That's when we entered the world of Android and got into Google Play and Amazon. At that point we were in 3 markets with 3 apps in each of the markets.

And at that point came December of 2011, where I was able to go from $200 USD in the last month to $600+!

Okay so this alerted me to the first really cool thing which I learnt early on. It doesn't matter the TIME FRAME it takes to make an app! You could just as easily make as much money from an app that takes a day to an app that takes nearly a year!

Secondly I realized that more apps means more money! As you can see from that example I was able to easily triple my revenues from 3 apps in 3 marketplaces!

Fast forward to today where we now have over 25+ apps in over 10+ marketplaces using some of the most amazing cutting edge money making techniques for monetization and well you do the math! By the way, I also learnt something really cool as well about various marketplaces. Each market place has a TOTALLY different way to make money and after I started learning how each market place worked, I have been able to successfully capitalize on those various markets!

I truly believe that I failed on that first app just so that I could write about it in this book today and help the thousands of upcoming developers out from making the same mistakes I did in the past!

Now after doing this for quite some time, I've now been able to set up a business that makes me money even while I sleep! I have only myself and God as my boss and I get to live an extraordinary life!

I do this full time, and I totally love what I do! In fact just recently from all the blessings of success I've been able to get, I decided to finally go and buy a car I've always wanted since I was young. I went out and got myself a beautiful blue-grey Mercedes C230 with a beautiful wood interior and cream colored leather seats! Having a strong Faith and having a reason that was so powerful is what really helped me to stay in the game!

Here I am now getting interviews, speaking at various events around North America and living the life most people dream of! So I can assure you that it is quite possible to make it in this business without having to build the next Angry Birds app! I love the fact that I can spend time with my family, travel anywhere in the world at any time, be my own boss and get paid while I sleep! But don't get tempted to believe that this is something that just happens overnight.

Take my own experience as your guide and understand that for many who have made it successfully in this business, it took years to do, and it is not something that you just automatically make money from (*EVEN THOUGH OVERNIGHT SUCCESS IS POSSIBLE, it is not a realistic expectation!*). Apps have lifecycles, trends, seasons and require a lot of marketing skills along with programming skills.

Over time I have been developing many tools and methods that also make this process faster and I have started releasing these same tools that can help new and existing app developers save hours on end as well as thousands of dollars in the app business!

I urge you to come visit my website at http://www.gamescorpion.com and click on the App Trillionaires link on the top. Use the special code **onetrillion** to access the special page I've made just for those who have read my books or have been part of my programs and use my tools. There you will find a constantly updated list of some amazing tools and resources available to you. At the same time you can even join up to one of my many paid programs that I'm constantly bringing out for app developers and app business owners and you can even purchase some of my more extensive tools right there as well! While you're there, sign up to my newsletter where I am constantly bringing out the latest news, tips and tricks and tutorials on the latest cutting edge methods to make even more money and monetize your apps!

The app world changes DAILY and keeping up to date on things is what will help you to succeed in this business! You can even join up our Facebook page and if you join one of our ongoing membership packages, you can even join me on one of my live web seminars. In these seminars we all interact and get to learn from each other and I go over some of the great new tips and tricks and tools that I have been learning consistently as well as going over answering questions. I'll also go over some techniques and methods that have helped myself and others to succeed in this businesses! I highly recommend it!

If you still need a reason to become an app developer, simply do a web search on mobile app success stories and you'll read thousands and thousands of successful app business owners living the dream! There is no limit to how much you can make in this business except for the limits you put on your self! I've said it already and I'll say it again, this is a ***business*** that requires your efforts and is not a get rich quick scheme that you just do for one week and forget about. It takes months if not years to make this a success, however if you create a solid base, follow my mentoring, keep up to date on the subject and stay on top of things, you can live the life people only dream of! Listen, you need to understand that this business changes fast! What worked in 2008 does not work now! What works now may not work 1-2 years from now! It changes constantly and you need to keep up with it in order to stay successful in this business.

APP BUSINESS MODELS

That being said, lets go onto some of the various app businesses models you can follow. You really need to think about which category you fall under before you even start an app business at all. Luckily I have created a nice little chart that you can take a look at that breaks down the various app business models (Image 1).

Image 1: Various App Business Models

As you can see there are several options available to you. Do you want to sell to end users just inside of app stores or do you want to sell apps to local businesses? Do you want to make apps for other APP Business Owners who would outsource your services or are you planning to work for a company as an app developer?

Depending on what you choose, you may have to agree to non-compete laws and regulations. The best (but most challenging way) to get in is as an App Developer to MASS CONSUMER. The other areas require more legal aspects and contracts in place such as NDAs (Non-Disclosure Agreements) or non-compete contracts.

APP TYPES: NATIVE, WEB AND ADHOC

Mobile Apps are broken down into 3 Distinct Categories:

1. NATIVE APPS: These are apps that run directly on a device and can run with or without an internet connection. You will usually find these types of apps in an app marketplace such as the Apple App Store or Google Marketplace. This is the MAIN type of app people try to create, but it's harder to get it approved.

2. WEB APPS: These apps run in a web browser and do not require any approvals. Using various forms of monetization, these apps can also make you some money as well, but they require a constant internet connection to run.

3. AD-HOC APPS: These apps are usually made for corporations and agencies that use apps internally. These are the same native apps from above, however they are not part of the App Store and can be sold on their own. It's basically a NON-PUBLIC Native App.

The path that I will be training you on is the best and most challenging one which is becoming an App Developer and selling your native apps via app stores to Mass Consumers. Other programs and books may recommend selling to local businesses owners which is also an excellent way to start.

However, if you were planning to work for another company making apps for them, then I would not really recommend that unless you are really desperate and get a solid offer. The reason is that you could very well make the next hit app that could sell millions of copies and the sad reality would be that you would not be getting anything but your base pay from it. If you do choose this path, always try to include some form of royalties from the app so that you make money as well from the number of units sold and not just the base pay for making the app as an employee.

Okay so that's enough on the App Business and getting you introduced into it. I didn't want to bore you with a whole bunch of statistics on the industry which you can easily find via a simple Google search. Suffice it to say that the mobile app industry is booming and expanding exponentially. Get on board now and start making money before time passes by and you are left sitting far behind the rest! You very well could become the next App Trillionaire!

"Ask, and it shall be given you; seek, and ye shall find; knock, and it shall be opened to you."

— Jesus

4. STARTING YOUR APP BUSINESS

I have setup much of this book to be in a step-by-step format with little notes and tips as well as possible costs you may incur in each step in US Dollars. Since many of you may be in a different point in the business, please choose to start where you believe you are. For many this may be a new first step, and it is exciting, and so I would recommend that you start here at the beginning. For others who have a running app business, you may want to start at another part, possibly looking into ASO or some of the various techniques and methods I have outlined in later chapters. For those who wish for more or may require some additional help, you may want to join one of my many training programs I am constantly building online for new and current app developers. Simply visit http://www.gamescorpion.com to view many of our trainings and while you're there make sure to sign up to my newsletter where I am always outlining the latest information and news on the mobile app business as well as providing tips and advice on the industry which I highly recommend!

In addition to this I have setup a Facebook page for those who have read the App Trillionaires book and are part of my programs or are in the mobile industry. I like to hold mastermind meetings every now and again, which really takes you to the next level, where you can meet like minded individuals who are also trying to learn and grow their own app businesses. You can join the group by visiting http://www.facebook.com/AppTrillionaires.

So lets begin with the first steps in starting your new successful App Business!

TIP: I highly recommend actually taking action on the steps I have outlined. If you need to do one step a day that is fine, but at least put it into a calendar and start taking action on it. I cannot stress how many potential app developers fail due to not taking action! If you really want to create a successful app business then you need to take ACTION!

STEP 1: Choose Business Model And Company Name (COST: $0)

a. Choose a business model from the business models I showed you earlier.

b. Choose a company name.

TIP: Keep your company names simple and memorable!

c. Check online to see if your company name and domain name are available. When I first started I used something like GoDaddy.com or Misk.com to view what domain names were available. I would also recommend a Google search to see if the company name you may be looking for exists or not. By making sure your company name is not available you can save yourself a lot of headaches and lawsuits in the future. In fact it took me nearly 2 weeks to really come up with a solid company name and a lot of research, and I finally settled on Game Scorpion. I also had Game Torch in mind at the time, however there was another several places that had that name so I finally chose Game Scorpion and went full force with it.

d. Decide on what business type your company is. Are you an individual (Sole Proprietor)? Do you want to protect your assets and plan a larger undertaking (Corporation)? Whatever you are planning to do will determine how long things take to setup. A sole proprietor for example can be setup on Apple App Store in a day or less whereas a Corporation (Like what I have) can take you three weeks or longer to get approved. If you are not sure, I would recommend talking to a lawyer or accountant who may be versed on advising you on the benefits of what type of company may work better for you.

STEP 2: Open The Business (COST: $60 to $2,000)

a. This week go to your local city hall or business development office to learn how you can open a business. You will be required to pay about $60 to $2,000 depending on which type of business you open. Sole Proprietorships tend to cost much less than corporations so figure out what works best for you and your budget. For me I knew this was my long term business and what I was planning to do full time always so I chose to open a corporation. It cost me personally around $500 in Canada to open the corporation online and pay for a names search.

STEP 3: Website and Domain (COST: $100-$300 / Year)

a. Go to GoDaddy.com or Misk.com and reserve your domain name for your business there for about $10-$20/year. I personally chose a .COM address over any other one due to the fact that a .COM is much more prominent when compared to other domains.

b. Next choose a web hosting service to host your website for you. This could cost you between $80-$200/year. GoDaddy.com offers many basic hosting packages. I personally use Exabytes.com for our hosting package as I find them affordable and more importantly, reliable.

c. For the website I setup a Word Press installation (www.wordpress. org) and obtained a theme for easy website management. There are many places to obtain word press themes such as ThemeForest.net, ElegantThemes.com and TemplateMonster.com.

TIP: If you have trouble in setting this up, simply head on over to www. fiverr.com and outsource the website for just $5! That's right, one of the nice little tricks we use in the industry is that we try and outsource what we can. Fiverr.com offers many providers who will install and setup your basic word press installation for a low price and you can be up and running easily by simply providing your web hosting details to a service provider. Make sure to change your passwords and access information after they set things up successfully.

d. Take a quick crash course tutorial on how to update and edit your new website and theme. You can find many of these tutorials online by doing a simple Google search or even searching Youtube videos.

STEP 4: Bank Accounts (COST: $10-$20 / Month)

a. This week focus on getting a bank account setup SPECIFICALLY for your business. Even if you are running a Sole Proprietorship, you still should have a separate account for your business. Many banks offer business bank accounts for around $10-$20 per month. In my case as I am considered an International App Developer being in Canada, I had to setup two accounts, one for Canadian Dollars and one for American US Dollars. I set these accounts up for around $15/month per account. When you sign up to app stores in the future steps, you'll be required to provide this information to them so that they can pay you via direct deposit.

STEP 5: Hardware and Services (COST: Up To $1000-$3000)

TIP: To truly keep your business mobile, purchase development devices that are mobile as well, such as Laptops instead of Desktops.

a. APPLE DEVELOPMENT

Apple Development will require you to purchase a Mac computer system. The Mac must be capable of running the latest version of xCode which means it must most likely be an Intel based Mac computer. Doing a simple Kijiji, Craigslist or local Classified search should yield you many people who are selling their old used Macs for cheaper prices. I was able to work out a deal when I first started and scored a sweet Macbook Air 13 Inch for just $800! Look around and see where you can save your money. The Mac system alone can cost you up to $2000 or more depending on what system you are planning to buy for your development purposes. Another option is to purchase a PC only and use a service called Mac In Cloud (http://www.macincloud.com). Mac In Cloud basically is a Mac computer you can use through the Internet that allows you to submit your app to Apple without requiring a physical Mac computer. This will cost you up to around $50/month to use this service, so it's a great option for new developers on a budget.

b. ANDROID DEVELOPMENT

For Android Development you will require either a Mac or Windows based system. You can easily purchase very powerful PC Windows Based Laptop system at your local electronics store for around $500. I purchased my laptops for example from Best Buy and Futureshop here in Canada.

The tools I will be recommending for development in this book will be heavily PC and Windows based. Having a solid PC Windows laptop then will be very important for your business.

c. Internet is a REQUIREMENT for this business to run successfully. Sign up for a constant high bandwidth internet connection. You want to be able to upload and download a lot of data without limitations. Most basic monthly internet packages should suffice. In Canada I pay around $40/month for High Speed Internet. This should be comparable to most places around the world. Having a solid internet connection is something that I just can't stress enough! MAKE SURE YOU HAVE IT!

d. Obtain testing devices to test your apps out. I would recommend to purchase at least one Android device and one Apple device. I personally have an iPhone, iPad and a Google Nexus 7 Android Tablet. You can purchase what you feel would help you the most. I have found that I can purchase tablets and phones easily via Kijiji and Craigslist for relatively low prices. I've been able to personally obtain Tablets for as low as $150! Whenever possible, save your money as there are a lot of expenses to get this business up and running.

STEP 6: Sign Up To Various App Markets and Setup Various Accounts (COST: $150-$300)

TIP: Make a special place in your web browser bookmarks section to start putting all the links you come across for your app business. There are a lot of websites and tools you will find along the way so always keep a list so you have easy access and wont forget!

a. Apple App Store

You will need to sign up as a developer by visiting http://developer. apple.com/programs/register/. You want to sign up to the iOS Developer Program and not the Mac Developer Program unless you plan to make Apps for Mac Computers specifically. The cost will be around $99/year to be an Apple App Developer.

b. Google Play Android Market

Visit https://play.google.com/apps/publish/ to sign up to Google Play

Market so you can develop for the main Android Marketplace. This will cost you about $25 as a one time fee by Google.

c. Other Markets

The following other markets I have personally tested and highly recommend. Please make sure to sign up for an account on these if you can. Not all of them are available to all countries and regions however these are the ones that I have tested with great results compared to others. There are literally dozens of market places out there for the Android market and only ONE for the Apple market. I personally use the tool ShiVa 3D to make my apps so I can program my apps once and then port them over to many markets without issue, even other alternate markets like RIM Blackberry, HP WebOS and several others. Over the years I have tested out many marketplaces and so the following marketplaces have been tested by me and have made me more money than others.

Alternate Marketplaces to Sign Up To:

    i.   Amazon (http://developer.amazon.com/)
   ii. Barnes and Noble (https://nookdeveloper.barnesandnoble.com)
  iii. Samsung (http://seller.samsungapps.com)
  iv. Blackberry RIM (https://appworld.blackberry.com/isvportal/)

d. Advertising and Monetization

The following places will allow you to monetize your apps and make money from placing ads within your apps or from sending push notifications. I have listed several places below, however keep in mind there are many more out there and will change over time. This is what has been working for me thus far, however as time goes on this list will change and so I highly recommend to always keep up to date on the latest trends, tools and market news to know what's the latest and greatest in app monetization. I have personally tested out the following and at this time I can personally highly recommend them. Please sign up and setup accounts at the following places:

    i.   RevMob.com (http://www.revmob.com/)

ii.   AdMob.com (http://www.admob.com)
iii. LinkShare.com (http://www.linkshare.com)
iv.   PushWoosh.com (http://www.pushwoosh.com)
v.   PushWizard.com (http://www.pushwizard.com)

e. Business Administration

I would highly recommend signing up to the following places and creating accounts which will help you run your business better. I personally have connected up all my emails to Gmail online which allows me to send and receive email from anywhere in the world on any device I want, thus truly making my business mobile! You'll definitely want to setup Gmail and Google Docs online using the links below as well as Google Calendar.

i.   Google Gmail (http://www.gmail.com)
ii.   Google Docs (http://docs.google.com)
iii. Google Calendar (http://www.google.com/calendar/)
iv.   Warrior Forum – For Marketing (http://www.warriorforum.com/)
v.   Reuters Daily Tech News (http://www.reuters.com/news/technology)
vi.   App Annie (http://www.appannie.com)
vii. Top App Charts (http://www.topappcharts.com)
viii. AppCod.es (http://www.appcod.es)
ix.   Fiverr.com (http://www.fiverr.com)
x.   oDesk.com (http://www.odesk.com)

! NOTE ! – The steps outlined thus far should take you about a week to accomplish. Schedule a good week or possibly two to get everything done. Do not move onto the next steps unless you are absolutely sure you have already setup your basic environment and all required membership fees and license fees to be an app developer.

"Never leave that till to-morrow which you can do to-day."

— Benjamin Franklin

5. OUTSOURCE OR DEVELOP?

So now that we have completed the first steps and setup a whole bunch of accounts and setup our business and have now got things running, we now need to actually create our first app.

There are two main ways to create an app. The first is to build it yourself by either using a special tool to make your app or learn programming. The other is to outsource development to others around the world.

Many people who are new to the app business will often ask this question: Do I learn to develop myself or do I outsource?

My programs specifically focus on learning to develop yourself, and the tools and software I am bringing out constantly and recommending in my programs will allow you to do just that by following along with my interactive tutorials which once again you can find on my website at http://www.gamescorpion.com.

Lets first go over outsourcing so you understand a bit more about what it is. After that I will go over developing yourself. Outsourcing may be a great option for those who may not like programming as much however I still recommend you learn some form of programming. Maybe take a crash course on programming online or at your local community college.

If you know nothing of programming, then many of these outsourced service providers may end up charging you a lot more money, and you may even have many project delays because you'd end up approving things incorrectly due to a lack of knowledge of common programming and technological terms. Suffice it to say that not knowing anything about programming will COST YOU!

OUTSOURCING OVERVIEW

From the previous steps we already setup two accounts on two highly recommended outsourcing websites. The first is Fiverr.com which is known for Micro-Services and the second is oDesk.com which is for larger projects like Apps and Websites.

Lets go over some of the pros and cons of outsourcing and some of the things you may run into just like I did when I first started outsourcing. This will save you a lot of time and headache by knowing this stuff upfront before even starting.

Firstly understand that when you are just starting out, your funds are going to be VERY limited. In fact as I said earlier, in order to run this business, you need to have a lot of apps, and a small budget will NOT allow you to outsource an amount of apps that generates enough revenue to cover your costs. For this reason I train new app business owners to become app developers first, and then later as their business grows, outsource to help grow even more.

I personally have outsourced several staff members as the business has grown and as things have become more challenging to handle just myself. However I still refuse to outsource my development to people I cannot trust as I don't want my ideas stolen, but that's just me. Even with all the NDAs (Non-Disclosure Agreements) in place, if someone really wants to steal your idea, they are going to steal it, and it's a big challenge and quite costly to start taking legal action over it (especially if the app is not a hit app anyways!).

HOWEVER what I like to do is split up the work into parts and hand it off to totally different outsourced staff so that even if someone had the intention to steal, they would require ALL assets of the app to really create the app, and that's one method of deterrent along with regular NDA agreements.

So now onto the Pros and Cons of Outsourcing!

PROS OF OUTSOURCING

a. Less upfront learning
Usually outsourced workers handle all programming and technical

details, so you can get up and running relatively fast rather than spending time learning programming.

b. Low cost of hourly staff compared to in-house staff
Outsourced staff can be as low as $1/hour depending on what needs to be done. You can also get the top of the line developers from Eastern countries for around $5-$10/hour.

c. No need to worry about common physical staff related issues
Outsourced workers are usually considered contractors. This means you won't need to worry about health benefits, hours of work, lunches, etc. Many of them work a minimum of 5 days if not 6-7 days a week and you won't need to worry about them as you would with physical employees. There is no physical office to open up daily and you can access your employees online from anywhere in the world.

d. 24×7 capabilities
Many of the outsourced service providers work while you are sleeping, thus giving you the benefit of a possible 24x7 operation. If you hire several outsourced service providers, you could have a full 24x7 operation with all the bells and whistles!

e. Automation
Yes the magical item I talked about earlier that doesn't FULLY exist. You can't automate everything, however you can automate several parts of this business to make your life easier and that's where outsourcing has its real strength.

f. Faster Hiring and Firing than regular in-house employees
One of the great benefits of outsourcing is the fact that you can hire fast and fire fast. If you don't like a contractors work, simply end their contract and hire another one. oDesk.com makes this fast and easy. No need for 2 week notices or uncomfortable situations. And most of the staff on oDesk end up finding more work through oDesk anyways as it is an open market. Rest assured you'll always be able to get top talent without risking a lot of your time and energy.

CONS OF OUTSOURCING

a. Language Barriers

Not English specifically, but more about how English is spoken. Words and cultural rules are very different in other parts of the world.

b. Technical Barriers

Trying to explain to outsourced staff what you want will be a CHALLENGE and can take a lot of time. You may ask them for example to make a ladder, they may in turn create something different that just raises you higher off the ground but is not the same thing as a ladder. This is a common downfall of outsourcing and can cause a lot of confusion and lost hours.

c. Longer creation times

Creation times are longer due to either the outsourced developers having more projects, or the fact that there is a lot of back and forth communication to get things done.

d. Loss of developers over time

Over time you may loose important developers who either take on too much work, find higher paying companies or just leave you without a reason. Full apps can be deemed dead at this point as there is no code to update them and original developers who know the code or have the code no longer work for you. You're left with a final version of an app that you either downgrade to a lower price due to no more upgrades, make free for helping grow your business, or take it off the market if the bugs are too problematic.

e. Management Issues

If you are not constantly keeping up with your outsourced staff, they tend to take a lot of time and in some cases stop working on the project. Always keeping up to date with your contractors is an important part of outsourcing.

f. Creativity issues and Quality Issues

Its no secret that outsourced work in general is of a lower quality than local and in-house employees. The only way to counteract this is to try and keep certain parts of the development IN-HOUSE or to outsource only to higher quality higher cost providers. For example you may want to outsource graphics to a dedicated Graphic Designer rather than leaving that up to the outsourced app developer.

g. Long term costs for many apps is ASTRONOMICAL!
One app alone will cost between $1500-$5000 realistically for a half decent app. Yes there are times you could get lucky and score a developer who may do something for $300 but those cases are rare if non-existent. In order to really do well in the app business you need to have many apps. If you outsourced that development that could run you into thousands if not HUNDREDS OF THOUSANDS!

h. Data Security
Possible loss of sensitive and important company data and information is a very real issue. Always be careful when handing out passwords and important company information as every now and again there are scam artists out there looking to do damage.

i. Idea Stealing and Loss
This one happens all the time! Possible loss of company secrets and app ideas! NDA Agreements are written to try and protect you from this very bad practice, however it is a very real issue that does happen and the only way to protect against this is to either develop yourself for the maximum security of your idea or to break apart the outsourcing so as to make it harder for someone to create the exact same app.

j. Lack of Dedication
As many outsourced staff work with many customers, your projects may not get the full 100% attention they need!

k. Confusing Non-Disclosure Agreements (NDAs)
Having to write and read very confusing Non Disclosure Agreements (NDAs) that may or may not work well in protecting your ideas depending on where in the world you are outsourcing to is a real downfall sometimes to outsourcing.

l. Sex Differences
I know this one seems kind of unusual, but trust me I learnt this first hand. Firstly if you are dealing with female employees around the world, in several cases I've had it be a ploy to hire their husbands or to try and

gain work for OTHER contractors. Secondly if the female outsourced staff member was genuine, then cultural differences were an important factor. For example I remember one time I hired a PHP Developer from India who was female to help us in updating our website page. Because I asked her how her day was going, which is a common practice in North America to simply be kind and ask your staff how they are doing, she instantly quit stating that I was trying to court her! Sometimes sex related (Like male/female interaction) or cultural related issues can come up and can cause issues when working with staff from around the world which is another reason why outsourcing is a challenge.

m. Cultural Differences

Another experience I had was with another worker whom I simply asked for their opinion on one of the ideas I had for my website at the time. They instantly thought me incompetent to lead and ended the contract! Apparently where this contractor was from, if a manger or boss ever asked for a personal opinion from a staff member, then that manager or boss was not capable of leading. WOW what a difference! Where that contractor was from, every boss or leader ALWAYS apparently had all the answers and knew exactly what they wanted and that's just the way it was. No one was entitled to an opinion other than the leaders. SO as you can see, you'll be having a lot of cultural issues as well to deal with, so think about this when hiring as well. Where in the world you hire and who you hire can be factors in success in your business. Unfortunately we don't all live in North America and cannot assume that it's the same worldwide.

n. Technical and Other Unusual Differences

Technically speaking, contractors in India and China and other parts of the world do not have the benefit of 24x7 power that we are blessed with here in North America. We also have the benefit of safety from our local communities. I've had some of my own outsourced contractors have terrorists in their local areas and their internets go down or they weren't allowed out of the house due to a state or city wide lockdown and curfew! I've also dealt with contractors who have had lower hardware systems to work with, such as slower computers or slower internet speeds. Other things for example are things like holidays, which in other parts of the world are much more frequent than in North America. Knowing that this exists will help you in your outsourcing expectations.

TIP: When outsourcing, go with an open and realistic mind with the new found knowledge you have just learned. Outsourcing is not perfect and requires some getting use to, however if done correctly can help you out in your business. I've noticed that the best priced English speakers who have some decent form of English capabilities come from the Philippines, where as those who have the most technical background are usually from India and China. I've also found that the most affordable and higher quality graphic designers tend to come from European countries. And of course the best and most expensive outsourced staff are from North America. Those are just my results and my own opinions at this time, however this is always changing and shifting so always keep up to date on the outsourcing market. A good thing to do before hiring any worker is to always see their portfolios and any reviews they may have had from other employers as that is always a solid indication of how good a contractor is.

SELF DEVELOPING OVERVIEW

Learning how to develop yourself is a challenge but also has the most cost savings and benefits for you in the long run. I highly recommend taking this course of action instead of outsourcing to start your business because you'll learn hands on what your business is about. Just as there is no Captain of a ship who does not know every part of their ship, as a business owner it is your responsibility to know your business inside out. The best way to do this is to develop things yourself and over time from the money you earn, re-invest it into processes and procedures to start automating the process more. Not only will this help you at the beginning in keeping your costs down, it will also help you in the long run when you do start outsourcing as you would already know what goes into getting an app into the various app stores and how to program them.

However like I said earlier, I highly recommend this option, but it is nonetheless a recommendation. Let me go over the pros and cons so you can decide for yourself if this option is for you. I personally however highly recommend this course of action over outsourcing when you are just starting out.

PROS OF DEVELOPING YOURSELF

a. Minimal Costs in the long run
You can create as many apps as you have the time to create without worrying about price issues or contractor delays.

b. No issues about others stealing your ideas
Hence no need for extensive NDAs (Non-Disclosure Agreements) as you are the only person touching the code and creating the base idea. Your ideas are protected by you and have less chance of being stolen.

c. Control over your own code
No issues of others re-using your code for other apps.

d. YOU GET the actual code, not just an app
This way you don't have to worry about developers leaving you hanging where you cannot update your apps. You'll always be able to not only update your apps but can also reuse your code to create even more apps!

e. Speed of creation
Everything gets faster with code reusing and there are no delays or higher costs for speed. As fast as you can code, is as fast as you can create. Various tools even exist that have a faster creation speed, but you don't have to wait on other developers to get code to you. You also don't have to worry about the back and forth hassle of trying to explain to other developers just exactly what you want. You can create EXACTLY what you envision rather than getting something that isn't quite what you wanted.

f. No scams
No worrying about being over charged or scammed by shady app development firms who are taking you for a ride due to your lack of knowledge or experience.

CONS OF DEVELOPING YOURSELF

a. Time to Learn How To Program

Possibly up to six months just to learn how to develop apps on your own.

b. Upfront cost of software, tools and hardware

It costs money to become a developer, and the software and tools required as well as the licenses can cost several hundred if not a few thousand dollars initially. In my opinion however it's well worth the investment for the long term gain you'll achieve, but once again it's my own opinion on it.

TIP: Use tools and methods that help to speed up the development process whenever you can. If you visit my website you can even sign up to my various programs and even purchase and obtain my special tools that I have available to help you in creating apps faster or in helping you run your app business much more easily. Once again the website is http://www.gamescorpion.com so check it out and sign up to the newsletter for up to date information on the app business.

"Learning without thought is labor lost."

— Confucius

6. STEP 1: APP RESEARCH

PART 1: WRITE DOWN APP IDEAS

As you are looking for various app ideas using the following methodologies, make SURE you have a paper and pencil handy to write them down! We will be going over the list AFTER you have created the list! Simply go through all theses steps and write down various app ideas as they come to you. The longer the list, the more options you'll have when finalizing on an app to create! I even built a simple app to help you generate some ideas called Easy App Idea Generator! You can find the link by visiting my website at http://www.gamescorpion.com.

a. Look for ideas via app stores!

Going over the Top 100 apps (PAID AND FREE) in the various app stores, Look for what's been selling for quite some time, non-FAD apps, non-HOLIDAY apps, etc.

I.   iTunes
    a.   iTunes Paid Top 100
    b.   iTunes Free Top 100

II.   Android
    a.   Android Paid Top 100
    b.   Android Free Top 100

III.   Amazon
    a.   Amazon Paid Top 100
    b.   Amazon Free Top 100

IV.   Barnes and Noble
    a. Barnes and Noble Paid Top 100
    b. Barnes and Noble Free Top 100

V.   Blackberry
    a. Blackberry Paid Top 100
    b. Blackberry Free Top 100

b. Look for ideas using LIFESTYLE (NICHE APPS)

I.   Target various lifestyles using Keyword Combinations
    a. KEYWORDS (Mom, Dad, Single Female, Single Male, Teen, Tween, Toddler, Senior) Come up with as many KEYWORDS as you can to help think of even more ideas. Ex. Divorcee, Newlywed, Newborn, etc.
    b. COMBINE WITH (Daily Routine, Work, Fun, Hobbies, Relaxation Time, etc.) Come up with as many COMBINING keywords as you can to think of even more great app ideas. Ex. Doing Groceries, Walking the Dog, Going on Vacation, etc.
    c. HOW TO USE: Example →
    An app for "Mom" who is "Doing Groceries" OR
    An app for "Single Male" to help them with "Hobby" X OR
    An app for a "Tween" for use during their "Vacation"

c. Look for ideas using MARKETS

I.   Target various markets

    a. Each market segment is different. You have MANY markets available to target. For Example:
        i. Men
        ii. Women
        iii. Seniors
        iv. Children
        v. Religious (Christian/Jewish/Muslim/Hindu, etc.)
        vi. Groups (Boards of Trade/Chamber of Commerce/Non-Profit Organizations, etc.)

vii. Political Beliefs (Republican / Democratic / Liberal /
   NDP / Conservative, etc.)

viii.Transportation (Those with a car/Those who ride a
   bicycle/Those who walk)

ix. Disabled/Physically Challenged

x. MANY OTHER MARKET SEGMENTS, Think of
   some others you may know of as well.

d. Look for ideas using NEEDS ANALYSIS

I.   Look for various needs that various people in a group may
have. For example think about the needs of a young student who is in
High School. What would their day to day needs look like? How about
the day to day needs of Parents? An Employee at a job? A Job Hunter
looking for a job? A Business owner?

II.   Go over the DAY TO DAY challenges that these various people
may encounter.

   a. When they wake up, is there a need we can help take care
      of there?
   b. When they go for breakfast?
   c. When they commute to their location of work/play
   d. When they are serving their function in society (Working/
      Studying/Playing, etc.)
   e. When they commute back from work/play, etc.
   f. When then sit down for dinner
   g. When they Relax after their day or during their day
   h. When they go to the gym or exercise
   i. Before going to bed
   j. During sleep/rest
   k. OTHER outside of their daily routine events: Groceries,
      going to the mall, vacations, holidays, etc.

e. Look for ideas using EMOTIONS

I.   Many purchases for apps happen because of an emotional need
that is trying to be solved. Usually it's trying to change a NEGATIVE

EMOTIONAL response into a POSITIVE EMOTIONAL response. Before we list the various negative and positive emotional responses, keep in mind of what apps you can create or come up with to try and help change a response. EX. Emotion of Sadness to Happiness OR Emotion/Feeling of Confusion/Overwhelm into Focus and Grasping of a Situation.

II.   Emotions and their opposites[1]

   a. SADNESS/GRIEF → JOY
   b. DISGUST/HATE → LOVE
   c. FEAR → HOPE
   d. GREED/ENVY → GENEROSITY
   e. CRUEL/MEAN → SYMPATHETIC
   f. SHAME → PRIDE/CONFIDENCE
   g. ANGER/RAGE → GRATITUDE/THANKFULLNESS
   h. FAMILIARITY/HABITUAL → SURPRISE/AMUSMENT
   i. DISGUST → DESIRE
   j. PANIC/ALARM → CURIOSITY/INTERST

III.   You can continue building upon the list above, but the point is that if you can create an app that can take people from a Negative/Painful emotion to a Positive/Happy emotion you will have a definite hit on your hands. Think of the TOP apps that have made it, how do they take a person from a Negative/Painful state to a Positive/Happy state? Can you describe which specific emotional groups an app is working with from the list above? Using this can you think of an app idea that may work as well?

f. Look for ideas using KISS METHOD

I.   KISS stands for **K**eep **I**t **S**imple **S**tupid (KISS). If you keep your app idea simple and to the point and easy to use with a straight forward function, it will tend to generate more buzz and sales volume than apps that are too complex or hard to use or do not state what they are in general.

---

1 Obtained   from   Wikipedia   http://en.wikipedia.org/wiki/ Contrasting_and_categorization_of_emotions

II.   What are some SIMPLE apps that you can think of?

g. Look for ideas through CATEGORIES of the top Markets

I.   Go to the marketplaces of each of the top markets and look through the categories.

II.   Note down categories that have a SMALL amount of apps, yet a high amount of download volume (Simply click on the number 1 app in that category to see the total amount of downloads).

III.   An app category that has HIGH DOWNLOAD VOLUME (by checking app download stats) and a LOW AMOUNT OF APPS means—MONEY! (Less competition and greater app sales volume)

h. GO OUTSIDE AND HAVE SOME FUN!

I.   This is by far a very gratifying experience. Simply go outside and enjoy your day, and throughout the day, think of apps that you could create that would help you in your day. If you go out for a coffee, maybe you could make a "Burnt My Tongue" app that would be a fun novelty thing. Or for example you may go to the grocery store and say, "Hey wouldn't it be neat to create an app for counting calories in food?"

II.   Have fun with this idea and keep going out to relax and at the same time come up with app ideas during your day to day adventures!

PART 2: EDIT APP IDEAS LIST FROM PART 1

Okay so now that we have a list of ideas, lets now organize them based on the amount of time, complexity and possible revenue. Rate the app ideas from 1 to 10 where 10 is the most hard, most complex app or LEAST revenue generating, and 1 is the easiest, least complex or MOST PROFITABLE app.

EXAMPLE TABLE:

10 → Worst rating

1 → Best rating

App Idea	Time To Create	Complexity (1 = Easy)	Revenue Potential

Step 1. Complete the Example Table using a Google Docs Spreadsheet or on regular paper.

Step 2. Zone in on a handful of apps (3-5 apps in total) that you would like to consider creating based on the best scores from the list above. (To calculate, just add the scores across and then rank them out of 30. 30 is the WORST rating and 3 is the best rating.)

Step 3. Create App Designs (Next Section) of the 3-5 app ideas. These designs will be used when creating the apps or when sending app ideas to developers to create.

"The best things are placed between extremes."

— **Aristotle**

7. APP ROYALTIES AND COPYRIGHTS

In this part we are going to go over several important definitions that you should know when it comes to app development and copyright laws. For more detailed descriptions you can always ask a lawyer for exact legalities surrounding your app as what we discuss here is a very basic overview.

ROYALTY FREE

If a person creates a work such as an image texture, a sound or a musical piece, they own the copyrights to that work. If you want to have the rights to use that work, you would talk to the original creator and pay them a FEE to use their work EVERY TIME the work was used. For example in a radio station, every time a song is played, the original artist would receive a royalty for the song being played. That is what a ROYALTY is in basic terms.

Royalty Free is being able to USE that same work AS MANY TIMES without having to pay any more ROYALTY to the original work creator. This you can think of as an unlimited usage license to use their work in your creations for personal or commercial use depending on how they have defined that usage.

This does not however give you any form of ownership on the creation of the copyrighted material. For example, you may buy yourself an iPad to use, however you are not the one who created the iPad. For this UNLIMITED/ROYALTY-FREE usage, you would usually pay an UPFRONT fee. Sometimes you can get royalty-free items for free as well.

When it comes to the world of software and apps, before you launch an app publicly you must make sure that you have obtained the Royalty-Free rights to use the IMAGES and SOUNDS that are incorporated into that very app.

This is very important because if in the future you have a HIT app and are using any copyrighted material inside of your app of which you have not obtained the Royalty-Free license to do so or own the copyrights yourself, you could end up being sued for damages.

Many times we may outsource our development to other developers or to artists without thinking about such things. Just because you have paid a developer for their TIME to create an app does not necessarily mean that you have paid for the usage rights of any images/sounds they may have used in your app.

Example—You hire Company XYZ from Overseas. Company XYZ is in a country that does not worry about Copyright or Digital Copying laws and so they simply find images through an Image search online and find sounds from various sources without worrying about the rights. Your app comes back and you have an image of a popular Movie Star with music in the background from a 1990's rock group. If you have NOT obtained the rights to use this content, you CAN and WILL be held liable.

OK So where do I get Royalty-Free items from that I can give to developers or use in my own apps?

Website 1. SoundSnap.com (http://www.soundsnap.com)
SoundSnap is a great resource for finding Royalty-Free sounds. You simply pay a fee of $9, $29 or one of their set fees, and you can gain access to various sounds ROYALTY-FREE. This is a great way to get music and sounds into your apps, from button clicks to entire Rock Ballads. SoundSnap is a great source of Royalty-Free material.

Website 2. CGTextures.com (http://www.cgtextures.com)
CGTextures is a great resource for _FREE_ ROYALTY-FREE Textures and images which can be used commercially in your apps. The only stipulation is that you may not use the images to sell individually or to

do any form of scrapbooking (please read the terms for more details). As for your apps this is a great site to gather ROYALTY-FREE images such as Clouds, Forests, Oceans and More!

TIP: Always research the terms and conditions of any websites you are planning to gain Royalty-Free items from. For your app development needs you need to have commercial usage royalty-free items.

"Faith is to believe what we do not see; and the reward of this faith is to see what we believe."

*— **St. Augustine***

8. STEP 2: APP DESIGN AND PAPER TESTING

In this step you will require a paper and pencil with an eraser. I usually use a mechanical pencil with lots of lead and a solid eraser. You can easily pick up these items in your local office store or dollar store.

For your photocopying purposes I have included a paper version of a mobile phone device I created on a separate page. Simply photocopy that page several times and cut out to start drawing your paper designs in the next part.

Also as a bonus if you visit my website at http://www.gamescorpion. com and click on the App Trillionaires menu link above, I will post up several documents there, including a special document called Phone Trace Paper which has 6 of the same mobile phone images so you can simply print it out, cut out the phone designs and start paper testing and designing your app! It's a free download available only to my readers and those who are part of my programs and use my tools. To access this special download page you will require the password: **onetrillion**. Feel free to sign up to our mailing list while there as well!

PHONE TRACE PAPER – SINGLE PHONE

Step 1: Paper Modeling (PROTOTYPING)

i.   Paper modeling is simply drawing out what your app looks like via paper and pencil.

ii. Create your app designs and then finally once completed scan them in if you wish to send them to a developer or save them for future.

iii. You can even take your prototyping and designing to the next level by buying various stencils and design tools by visiting UIstencils.com (http://www.uistencils.com/)

Step 2: Common Components in Apps

i.   Virtual Keyboard
ii.   Left/Right buttons
iii. Home Button
iv.   Drop Down (COMBO) boxes
v.   Radio Buttons
vi.   Checkboxes
vii. Text Boxes
viii. Sliders

Step 3: 80/20 rule

i.   If 20% of your labor can overcome 80% of your work, do the 20% labor first!

ii. In terms of an app, if you are developing an app with various functionalities, if you know that lets say it takes 5 minutes to develop an image for a clock background or 2 hours to program a clock image background, you're better off taking the faster 5 minute approach and moving on. You can easily update the app in the future to add more advanced functionality.

Step 4: KISS Method

i.   Same as before, Keep It Simple Stupid (KISS). When designing apps always keep your designs easy and simple. Even though you may have many complex ideas, it's the apps that can make these complex ideas EASY that hit off and gain major success.

ii. Usually try and keep an app (Especially those from more complex markets) SIMPLE and easy to use. The reason why GOOGLE hit off as a search engine was due to its SIMPLE interface. Just a SINGLE search box, you search for what you want. Other search engines were more complex, had all kinds of things to do, and many other areas that confused users. Today who do we know owns the entire search engine market without a doubt? GOOGLE. KEEP IT SIMPLE!

Step 5: FUN FACTOR AND TALK Method

i. When designing, ask yourself, "Would someone have FUN with this app?" or "Would someone show their friends and talk about this app?" Let me break it to you straight...IF NO ONE TALKS ABOUT YOUR APP, your app will not sell very well. Word of mouth is the most powerful method of marketing, and now even more so in the app world. We see it via App Reviews, but we also see it via PHYSICAL app sharing. You may see a friend using an app, or having fun with an app, and guess what, you just created a conversation starter right there. Always ask yourself if your app will either be fun, talked about or both!

Step 6: Easy online tools to help in Prototyping

a. iPhone Mockup Web App → http://iphonemockup.lkmc.ch/
b. Serena Prototype Composer → http://www.serena.com/products/prototype-composer/index.html
c. Rethink Realizer → http://www.realizerapp.com/
d. (TOP CHOICE) Just In Mind Prototyper → http://www.justinmind.com/prototyper/free-edition

PROTOTYPE AND PAPER TESTING ACTION STEPS

1. Start by photocopying and cutting out the amount of screens

you believe your app will have by using the Phone Trace Paper shown on an earlier page.

2. Draw out rough versions of your screens. Try and make your app functional. For example if you want to show a button, draw a rectangle, and then if someone was to click on that button, draw the screen that would show up after pushing that button.

3. After drawing out all the paper prototypes, start doing some paper testing. Put the slides in the correct order and get a friend or someone who you know to come and test the app out on paper. If they click on a button, show the next page that they would see by clicking on it. Paper testing is the fastest and cheapest way to really get your app idea off the ground.

4. Repeat this process for all of the apps you selected in earlier steps (Around 3-5 apps) and then once you have paper tested all the ideas, start scanning them in for actual creation.

5. At this point you are now ready to either outsource the app development to an overseas company or to build it yourself. Based on what you have decided, it is now time to put together all your assets and items.

"Sometimes a fall is the only way to rise!"

— Abhinav Gupta

9. STEP 3: CREATE THE APP

In this step you are required to do what it takes to start creating your app. If you are planning to outsource, then start outsourcing on oDesk for an app developer or app development company. Make sure you have written NDAs and have your materials and resources ready to give to the developers to start working.

Weigh your options carefully when just starting out! As your business grows, you will eventually have to convert over to the Outsourcing route, but to start with you may want to try your hand at developing yourself. Not only does this help you save some money upfront as you grow your business, but later in the future when other developers are quoting you prices on work, you will know what developer is taking you for a ride and what developer is not. Once again it comes back to SAVING MONEY!

Let's go over the outsourcing route here in a more detailed step by step method.

OUTSOURCING THE APP

STEP 1. CREATE THE AD
a. Outsourcing Websites for App Development

There are two main types of outsourcing websites available in the market; Regular Outsourcing and Micro-Service Outsourcing. Regular Outsourcing focuses on major projects that are large. The following are some very highly used outsourcing websites that are for major projects. On these sites you can set a budget size of any amount. I personally have used and can recommend oDesk, but I am listing others so you have some options as well.

http://www.guru.com
http://www.odesk.com
http://www.elance.com

TIP: I would highly recommend only sticking to regular outsourcing websites for your main app development. It is a very big mistake to go to micro-service outsourcing websites expecting a full app to be made for a cheap price. Remember, you get what you pay for at the end of the day!

b. Ad Basics

Create an ad on one of these sites that shows outsourced service providers what you are looking to have made. Do not put specifics or your app idea in the job posting unless you want to risk your idea being stolen! Your goal is to keep it simple, for example, "Looking for an app developer to make an Entertainment or Utility app" and then go into details on what you expect from a service provider. Whatever you do, do NOT put your exact idea there!

STEP 2. HOW TO SELECT AN OUTSOURCING SERVICE PROVIDER
a. Select a Service Provider

Selecting an outsourcing provider is based very similarly to any auction website. You simply see the feedback score and review previous work a service provider has done and then go from there. That's the first step.

b. Do an Interview

The second step is conducting an interview to basically check if everything that the service provider stated lines up in the interview. For example if they say they are fluent 10/10 in English and can communicate correctly, and you interview them and they can barely speak English, then they have just lied on the resume. This would be important for you if you were looking for someone who was going to MARKET YOUR

APP for example. In my case, I hired several people for creating press releases for me. This interview process helped me to weed out those who were just lying to get the gig versus those who were really genuine.

c. Probation Contract

The third step after all the items check out is to do a PROBATION contract first. This is simply a week or a few days or even a single hour or even a small project (Depending on what's being done), just to test the service provider. Before you go full force with a service provider, take a small budget for testing the provider out. You should do this with only those who have passed your interview. Take a small part of your budget to test out their skills. After this, make your final selection and complete your app. Always have one or two people as a BACKUP from the above steps, just incase a provider screws you over or you just decide you are not satisfied with the work.

After selecting a service provider, have them sign a Non-Disclosure Agreement with you (I recommend you speak with a lawyer or find guidance on how to create/obtain a NDA Agreement).

Before you begin to discuss ANY ideas with any service provider, always have an agreement signed by them. This may be hard to enforce in various parts of the world, but at the end of the day it shows the service provider that you mean business and that your idea is valuable.

TIP: This 3 Step method will in most cases get you a decent service provider who will give you the results you want. Finding a solid service provider can take YEARS! It is not an overnight ordeal! You are building a relationship with your developer, so do not expect to have this happen overnight.

KILLER OUTSOURCING TIPS

Here are some things to look out for when outsourcing to various parts of the world based on my own experiences.

a. The FURTHER EAST, the LOWER THE PRICE!
All Asian Countries are very low in price!

b. The FURTHER WEST, the HIGHER THE PRICE!
Euro/North American Countries are very high in price

c. The FURTHER EAST, the LOWER THE QUALITY!
This is generally true, but in some rare cases you end up getting a good solid app.

d. The FURTHER WEST, the HIGHER THE QUALITTY!
Once again this is generally true.

TIP: When looking to hire an outsourced service provider, rank them based on the following points:

  a. Price
  b. Estimated Time to Create app
  c. Feedback score
  d. Synergy (Who seems like they work well with you and can understand what you want more than someone else based on your interview?)
  e. Overall Quality of Output (How is the quality of output of the previous apps this service provider has made for others?)

MICRO SERVICE WEBSITES

Micro-service outsourcing focuses on services that have a lower cost to them. For example, most of the Micro-Service websites focus on a low fee per service rendered model. This means that for $5 or something as low as that, people are willing to provide you a specific service, from simple icon design to singing you a birthday song on youtube!

The most popular micro service websites are listed below:

http://www.fiverr.com
http://www.tenbux.com
http://www.gigbucks.com

SELF DEVELOPING THE APP

This is by far amongst the most challenging, yet the most rewarding option available in the app business. I highly recommend starting to develop yourself so that you start to learn the ins and outs of what goes into making an app and how to get your app into the app store.

I use a special tool to create apps across multiple markets called ShiVa 3D. ShiVa 3D is a state of the art 3D WYSIWYG (What You See Is What You Get) app and game development tool. Its greatest strength lies in its ability to port a completed app or game into various marketplaces without much recoding of your original app.

In fact I have created many tools and programs that revolve around ShiVa 3D that can help you in your app development and creation. It is however going to take you time to learn to develop using this tool and will require some form of programming knowledge and background.

Over the next several pages I will be going over a basic overview of ShiVa 3D so that you get a taste of this development environment and can start learning to develop your own apps.

However before you begin going down the ShiVa 3D road, let me point out that there are other options as well if you are looking for something less extensive when it comes to programming.

LIST OF APP CREATION AND DIY TOOLS
The following is a list of other development tools and websites you can use to create apps fast and easy:

*1. Appmakr.com (*http://www.appmakr.com/*)*
This website features codeless app creation for free based on creating web apps.

*2. GameSalad Creator (*http://www.gamesalad.com/creator*)*
GameSalad is a great WYSIWYG tool to create 2D Video Games for iOS and Android devices. It also features a very little/no-coding based system that you can use to start developing apps immediately.

*3. TapLynx (*http://www.taplynx.com/*)*
This is another codeless app development tool to create iPhone apps.

*4. MobileRoadie (*http://mobileroadie.com/*)*
Another app building website focusing on easy app creation.

*5. iTorque 2D GarageGames (*http://www.garagegames.com/*)*
A powerful set of tools to create games and apps for iPhone and iPad.

*6. PhoneGap (*http://www.phonegap.com/*)*
A mobile app building tool.

7. Unity 3D (http://unity3d.com/)
Another extensive tool like ShiVa 3D, however requires a lot more coding background.

So there you have several app and game development tools that you can use to start your own development of apps. I however would still recommend spending several months and learning ShiVa 3D development and programming as it will allow you to scale up as you grow. Not only will you be able to create basic 2D apps with ShiVa 3D but you can also build full high end 3D Video Games! The most important strength behind ShiVa 3D is its porting capabilities that will get you into more markets and hence, increase your profit potential!

KILLER SELF DEVELOPMENT TIPS
a. Not all programming tools are made equal
If you get something too simple, as you grow you'll end up being limited to the type of apps you can make and thus will have to re-learn something new just stay up to date. I would recommend learning a tool that will last you for a long time rather than a tool that will limit you in the future.

b. Keep reference material close at hand
If you can find a website which lists the documentation of the tool you use or common functions or programming reference items, then I highly recommend you have it all bookmarked! I personally have all the ShiVa 3D documentation bookmarked and close at hand whenever I need to find a specific code function.

c. Join forums and ask for help!
Always join the community forums of the tool that you are going to

use to create apps. You can always ask for advice or tutorials from other successful or more experienced developers. Joining a forum is always a great idea and will help you start the process of developing.

d. Search Youtube for Video Tutorials

This is a great way to learn new things and little tricks that people with experience may have placed on youtube. I can't tell you how many times I found great little golden nuggets on Youtube about development and programming in 3D when I was just starting out. If an image is worth a thousand words, a youtube video is worth infinite words! It can definitely save you hours of reading lengthy documents!

e. RE-USE Code!

After developing a few apps, re-use old code to speed up the app development process! You can end up creating apps in a fraction of the time by re-using your old code! I highly recommend it!

f. Don't give up!

Programming can be a challenge, but learning how to develop apps will help you understand what future developers you hire or outsource may be going through. You'll also learn the terminology well which will help you in running your business. Another great strength is that by knowing how to code and develop yourself, when new devices come out or when new technologies come out, you can be amongst the first early adopters to integrate and incorporate them and thus have a greater chance at increased profits!

SELF DEVELOPMENT: SHIVA 3D OVERVIEW

Let me start by giving you a quick introduction to the world of ShiVa 3D. You can start off by visiting http://www.stonetrip.com and get yourself a copy of the FREE web edition of ShiVa 3D. This will allow you to make apps for the web, but if you seriously want to develop commercial apps and games then I recommend purchasing the Basic version. Before you purchase however, first go through some of the basic tutorials and walkthrough and see if ShiVa 3D is right for you.

So What is ShiVa 3D and Why Should We Use It?

ShiVa 3D is a special software program that we use to develop apps and programs that run on computer systems and devices known as HARDWARE, such as an iPhone or an iPad. The term APP, as stated earlier, is a short form for the word **APP**lication which is the word we use in the computer world for a computer program. In order for a piece of HARDWARE to work, it needs Applications which are commonly referred to as Software programs. Software programs can be as large as an Operating System or as small as a simple calculator. Each program has a specific function that it must do on the machine or piece of hardware. If there was no software, the hardware would pretty much be a dead paper weight.

So Why Use ShiVa 3D?

Well there are many reasons for this as I have outlined below:

1. *Price vs other tools on the market!* ShiVa 3D is priced at around $400 USD for their basic version which gives you commercial creation capabilities.

2. *Ease of programming!* ShiVa 3D features LUA Scripting vs. much more advanced C/C++ or Java programming that other tools require.

3. *Portability!* ShiVa 3D allows you to develop ONE TIME, but export that same app to MANY platforms including, Windows, Mac, Linux, iOS (iPad, iPhone, iPod Touch), Android (Google Play, Samsung, Kindle Fire, Barnes and Noble Nook, etc.), Blackberry (Blackberry Playbook and even now the latest BB10 Platform), WebOS (Palm and HP Touchpad), and many more systems coming out all the time. It even allows you to get into the CONSOLE market and port full games over to Nintendo Wii, XBOX 360 and other popular consoles as well!

4. *No ADDITIONAL Fees for new markets!* The ShiVa team keeps coming out with new places you can port your app to. Just recently they brought out in BETA form, Windows Phone capability. You would not be paying for this as a developer

which is an ADDED bonus! A new market means a NEW POTENTIAL CASHFLOW and you won't have to re-code all your previous apps again! Simply use the ShiVa Authoring tool and your app will be ported to the new platform!

5. *Supportive Developer Forum.* Whenever you are stuck, having others who are also developing helping you out can save you a lot of time. ShiVa forums are a great place where all the developers work together to help each other out. This is a great way for you to be able to troubleshoot issues you may have within your apps.

SHIVA 3D ACTION STEP

Start off by downloading yourself a free copy of ShiVa 3D Web Edition and start trying out some of the many tutorials available to you as a new developer.

You can find some of the latest tutorials and walkthroughs for ShiVa 3D by visiting the ShiVa Wiki and clicking on Get Started: http://www.stonetrip.com/developer/wiki

Try making some small applications to start with, such as a simple button app, and then try and port it out to the various devices such as an iPad, iPhone or Android device if you have any. Once you know you can do this and test it out successfully, try creating a more advanced app and keep on upgrading your skills.

If after testing out ShiVa 3D you find that it is something that you believe would be of benefit, then I have a special offer for our readers and users of my books, app tools and programs for 10% off your purchase of ShiVa 3D. Simply visit the Stonetrip website at http://www.stonetrip.com and use the coupon code: **kaw3pRap**.

"Tears won't change your situation. Get up, move forward & make your dreams come true! Positive action yields results."

— Abhinav Gupta

10. IMAGE EDITING 101

Why do we need to learn how to use an image editor?

An Image Editor is a tool that we use on a computer system that allows us to edit and manipulate images. We can do basic things such as removing red-eye from photographs, to more advanced image editing such as creating masks and various digital effects. Image editing has been around for many years and has given many users the power to create, edit and modify photos and graphics in ways we never could before many years ago.

In the app business, we will be doing a LOT of image editing. Image editing is required from a Graphic Artist's point of view to create the Icons, Screenshots and other in-app elements that you will require for your apps. After that, you as the app developer/app business owner will require image editing to do simple changes or to approve graphics that are being sent to you by either other Developers, Outsourced Graphic Artists or other contractors who are on the project. Knowing how an image editor works, what are the functions and terminology and what things you can do will greatly help you in your future as an App Developer and App Business Owner!

If you visit my website at http://www.gamescorpion.com and go to the special App Trillionaires page (Use password **onetrillion**) you will find there a special document that I've created that will list to you many of the common image sizes for icons and screenshots. In your mobile app business you will notice that you will require different sizes for images and from my own experience I know how confusing trying to remember all the sizes for the various markets can be. This special document will outline the various screenshot and icon sizes from most of the major markets and I try my very best to keep it updated.

IMAGES AND COMMON TERMINOLOGY

As you get into the business, you will come across many common file formats that you will be constantly opening up and using for various things. The common formats you will see most of the time are listed below:

JPG, JPEG → Pronounced "JAY-PEG" this image format is the MOST common one. Usually you will get great quality mixed with lower size files in most cases. Because of this feature (Low File Size, Decent Quality Image) JPEG took off as the most common and popular image format on the web. The only limitation that you have with JPEGs is that they do NOT allow for transparencies/transparent pixels. This is a very important feature, especially for icons which have ROUNDED corners. Using a JPEG you would not be able to do such a thing.

PNG → PNG Files are similar to JPEG files however they ALLOW transparent pixels and can store more image information. For this reason they tend to be larger in size. PNG files however are required for most of the final uploading to various marketplaces. Specifically for ICONS PNG files allow you to use transparencies to make unusual shaped images, such as cutting off the corners for icons to give that rounded look. Many markets, including iOS, Barnes and Noble and several others will require some of their images in PNG format.

TGA → Pronounced "TARGA" these files are a little less common, however are usually used by graphic designers and we will specifically also see these image formats being used in ShiVa 3D. They hold a lot more information on an image such as the raw data information. For this reason, you will notice that their file sizes tend to be much larger.

PDF → Not a common IMAGE file format, but it is used every now and again for developers or graphic artists who may want to show you a proof of an image but to make sure you can GUARANTEED see it on your end, they save it in PDF format which allows you to either open in your image editor if it has the capability to open PDF or most likely Adobe Acrobat Reader.

GIMP – AN OPEN SOURCE IMAGE EDITOR

GIMP is an open source, free to download, image editor that has many powerful features and tools. I jokingly call it the poor man's Photoshop because it truly is that powerful and yet costs nothing to download! You can make some incredible looking graphics using this tool, and you can also edit a lot of different file formats. The best part of this tool is the fact that there are a lot of tutorials on the internet regarding it, and in many cases, most of the Photoshop tools are almost the exact same. Later in the future if you ever decide to turn to using a professional tool like Photoshop, you'll already have the basic skills you learn from GIMP which would make things that much more easier!

GIMP INSTALLATION AND SETUP

A. Go to http://www.gimp.org/downloads/

B. Click on "Download GIMP 2.8.0 – Installer for Windows XP SP3 or later" to download the file for windows.

C. Choose the Desktop as the location for the download and as the file is downloading, continue onto reading the next section.

IMAGE EDITING CONCEPTS

A.   DPI – Written as dpi
dpi Stands for Dots Per Inch. It is a measure used to determine how many dots of INK will be placed inside of a single inch. The higher this number is, the higher the quality of the image will be when PRINTED OUT PHYSICALLY. This also increases your image size and resolution as well. Usually for web purposes, the dpi is set to around 72 as a common amount, however when you want better looking graphics, higher dpi values are required. For our apps we will specifically be making all our graphics and icons in 300 dpi. You can also choose higher amounts, but for now we are keeping it at 300 dpi.

B.   Resolution
Resolution is the number of PIXELS across your screen by the number of PIXELS down the screen. A pixel is simply a single

dot of light that can change color. If you take a magnifying glass and hold it up to your computer or laptop screen, you should see MANY little squares or dots. These individual dots/squares are known as PIXELS. Images come in various Resolution sizes. Here are the COMMON image resolutions for ICONS and SCREENSHOTS:

ICON Resolution (COMMON):
512px by 512px or 1024px by 1024px

Screenshot Resolution (COMMON)
1024x768 (iPad screenshots)
1024x600 (Amazon screenshots)
800x480 OR 480x800 (Android Screenshots)

There are MANY OTHER screen resolutions based on the market you are aiming to put your apps into. You will find that you will require a list to track all the various app sizes.

C.   Layers
Take two sheets of paper. On one of them, draw a circle. On a second one, draw two dots for eyes and a smiley face in the same location as where the circle is on the FIRST sheet. Now hold both sheets together and hold it up to the light and you should see a FULL smiley face as a single image.

Each SHEET of paper in that example is considered a LAYER. Layers are an important part of image editing and can allow you to do things such as move objects around in front of backgrounds, or even simply hide layers to help you in image editing even more. The concept of layers will become more easier to understand as you start learning and using an image editor more.

NOTE: At this point we are assuming that you have installed GIMP. The next parts will all continue inside of the GIMP program.

GIMP Tools

Before I start going over this basic overview of GIMP, firstly I want to alert you that this is just a very basic overview of an image editor. If this stuff intimidates you, not to worry! When I first started learning this stuff, it also was quite confusing, however when you are dealing with graphic artists, knowing this stuff is essential! There are too many times in this business that you will be dealing with images, and the last thing I want you to go through is having a greedy graphic artist charge you a lot of money for something you can do yourself easily. Learning basic image editing for this rreason is important! I've seen people get charged for something as simple as SHIFTING THE LOCATION OF TEXT in an image to simply changing the color of a background! Some people have been charged hundreds of dollars for such simple changes to an image!

So suffice it to say, learning a basic amount of image editing can save you a lot of money in this business in the long run. Let's now take a look at GIMP and some of the tools it offers.

GIMP consists of several windows. One of the most used windows is the TOOLBOX. The toolbox has many tools that you will use frequently inside of GIMP. In the bottom listing I have BOLDED items that we use most often in image editing and also added a little explanation of them. Non-bolded items I will just list but I won't go into detail explaining their usage.

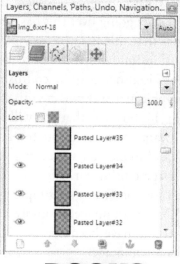

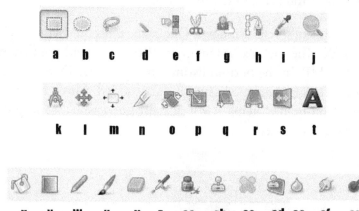

The GIMP Toolbox Window And Dock Window

From Top Left to Bottom Right the tools in the GIMP Toolbox are:

<u>MARQUEES (Marching Ants):</u>
a. **Rectangular Marquee Selection Tool**
This tool is used to select items that are usually in a rectangular or square shaped dimension.

b. **Ellipse Marquee Selection Tool**
This tool is used to select items that are usually in a circular or oval shape dimension.

c. **Lasso Marquee Selection Tool**
This tool is used to select irregular polygon style shaped items in an image.

d. **Magic Marquee Selection Tool**
This tool will speed up your selection process by selecting entire regions of a specific color.

e. Color Marquee Selection Tool

<u>OTHER TOOLS:</u>

f. Scissors
g. Foreground Select Tool
h. Paths Tool

i. **Color Select Tool**
This tool will allow you to set the foreground color to the color you select with this tool. It's really handy when trying to get the exact color of an icon or app.

j. Zoom Tool
k. Measure Tool

l. **Move Tool**
This tool will allow you to adjust and move a layer simply by clicking and dragging a layer while having this tool selected.

m. Alignment Tool

n. Crop Tool

o. Rotate Tool
This tool will allow you to rotate a certain image layer by a certain amount of degrees.

p. Scale Tool
This tool will allow you to shrink or grow a layer you select by a certain percentage.

q. Sheer Tool
This unique tool will allow you to stretch a layer in a special way known as Sheering.

r. Perspective Tool
This tool will allow you to stretch a layer to any dimension you want. I use this tool to help me in creating 3D screenshot effects for my app screenshots.

s. Flip Tool

t. Text Tool
This tool allows you to add text to your image.

u. Paint Bucket Tool
This tool allows you to fill a selected layer or a portion of a layer in the color of the foreground.

v. Gradient Tool
A gradient is a gradual color change from one color to another. It can really enhance the look and feel of icons and app screenshots. Use it to fill a certain region in your image with a gradual color that changes from the foreground color to the background color.

w. **Pencil Tool**

Use this tool to draw lines and dots and draw freehand.

x. **Paintbrush Tool**

Use this tool to paint with various brush head on the selected image layer.

y. **Eraser Tool**

Use this tool to erase mistakes.

z. Airbrush Tool

aa. Ink Tool

ab. Clone Tool

ac. Healing Tool

ad. Perspective Clone Tool

ae. **Blur Tool**

Use this tool to blur out parts of an image.

af. **Smudge Tool**

Use this tool to SMUDGE or push parts of an image around.

ag. Dodge/Burn Tool

GIMP Docks

In GIMP we will be navigating our image using various DOCKS. Docks are various windows that can allow us to view different aspects of our image. For example, we may want to view layers, and so at that point we open up the Layers Dock. We may also want to zoom in and navigate throughout the image, and for this we use the Display Navigation Dock.

Simply by clicking on the TINY ARROW next to the name of the Dock window you are in, you can add more dock windows to the list. The most common dock windows you will be using in GIMP is the Layers Dock and the Navigation Dock.

GIMP Selection Modes

Previously I outlined various MARQUEE (Marching Ant) selection tools. Each of these tools has various types of SELCTION MODES.

You can ADD to a selection, SUBTRACT from a selection, or even INTERSECT a current selection. Each method will allow you to grow or shrink your selection in a various way.

Once you have made your initial selection you can now Shrink or Grow it by the following methods:

To Shrink on the menu simply press Select→Shrink and select a pixel amount to Shrink by.

To Grow, on the menu simply press Select→Grow and select a pixel amount to Grow by. You will find this to be a very easy to use method to select various parts of your images.

Finally we have the MAGIC WAND Marquee tool. There will be times that you have unusual edges or even curves. A simple way to select objects is by using a RANGE of colors. This is where the Magic Wand marquee tool comes in handy and allows you to select various parts of an image simply by clicking on it. This can save you a LOT of time compared to other methods of selection.

GIMP Image Scaling/Transform/Crop

If we select a layer from our Layers Dock, we can simply HIDE/Make Visible the layer by clicking on the little EYE icon next to it.

In order to SCALE the layer, we simply select the Scale Tool and resize our image by simply clicking and dragging or even putting an image size.

To move our layer, we simply select our layer in the Layers dock and select the Move Tool. We then select on any active pixel in the layer and we will be able to move that layer to any location in the image canvas.

Finally if we use our Marquee tools, we can select an area and then select

Image→Crop To Selection, and the entire image will be shrunk down to the size of your selection.

FILLS AND GRADIENTS

Using the paint bucket, we can fill an ENTIRE area of an image with either a single color, or an image pattern. Simply select the Paint Bucket tool, choose a color from your colors list and then click on any area in the active layer you wish to have the color painted onto. Notice that the PAINT bucket will tend to fill in based on a region it finds via color or even an entire layer. If you use the Marquee tool, you can even force a fill in a certain location.

A Gradient is a fancy word for saying, "Draw colors from Color 1 to Color 2 in a smooth way". For example, If I want to go from Black to White, I would first start with Black and then continue onto all the other Grays until I reach White. It would just keep getting lighter and lighter as we get closer to the color white. Gradients are used to enhance an image and give it an added touch of DEPTH.

NEXT STEPS

I Highly recommend doing several tutorials or watching youtube videos and learning more about image editing basics. In a days time as an app developer I'm opening up the image editor at least 3 or more times! From Icons to screenshots to approvals of app designs, images are a very important part of the app business! Knowing how an image editor works and how to use it well will help you not only work with images easily and fast, but it may also save you some unnecessary costs which you could incur just from the lack of knowledge of image editing.

"Overnight success is many years of persistence... ironically when it happens, people say it's OVERNIGHT because they didn't know about you the night before!"

— Abhinav Gupta

11. THE APP LIFECYCLE

In order to market apps successfully, you must understand the app LIFECYCLE!

In general most apps that are launched tend to decline in popularity to a point where they can only be found via an app search, which is what I like to call **App Oblivion** because it is no longer in the charts. In general at this point, the app sales volume decreases greatly, when compared to the initial launch and thus it is only findable via an app search.

The app lifecycle in general goes through the following:

1. **Launch**

   The launch of an app can last anywhere from 1 to 3 weeks depending on how powerful you started your marketing. In general without marketing, chances are you'll hit app oblivion faster. Keep in mind, there are times with an app where an app may just hit oblivion immediately. That can be painful, so make sure you do some form of basic marketing (spread the word via social networks like twitter or facebook or on message boards, etc.) and try and increase the odds of a longer launch period.

2. **General sales gain and increase**

   As word starts to spread, if you did a good job and have a good app, then you should start to see sales rise over time. At any moment however as always, your app can hit oblivion, but an app can have a lifetime of around 1-6 months before it dies out into oblivion in general. Some apps don't reach oblivion for a long time and first hit what is known as Terminal Velocity or Plateau.

3. Terminal Velocity / Plateau

This is the point where everyone has learnt about the app or already has the app and is kind of getting sick of the app. Either the app is now outdated or is just no longer popular because everyone already has it. Angry Birds is currently in Plateau and is starting its decline now. Everyone either already has it or is getting sick of it and is just waiting for the next big hit. This stage is pretty much the HIGHEST sales you can expect for an app without any other forms of advanced marketing.

4. Decline

At this point the app is loosing its steam and heading right into Oblivion and there is pretty much no stopping it unless you start some advanced marketing techniques as I outline in Chapter 12.

General App Lifecycle

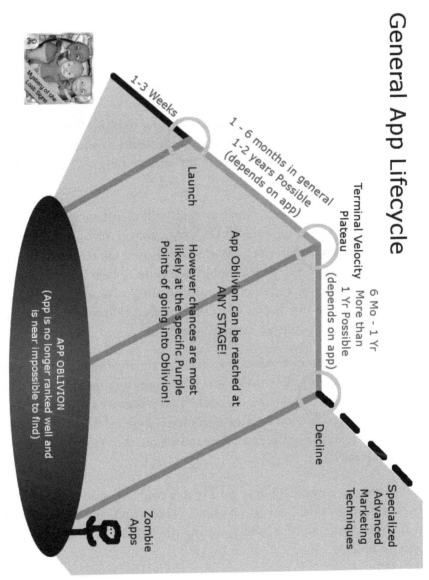

1-3 Weeks

1 - 6 months in general
1-2 years Possible
(depends on app)

6 Mo - 1 Yr
More than
1 Yr Possible
(depends on app)

Terminal Velocity
Plateau

Launch

App Oblivion can be reached at
ANY STAGE!

However chances are most
likely at the specific Purple
Points of going into Oblivion!

Decline

Specialized
Advanced
Marketing
Techniques

APP OBLIVION
(App is no longer ranked well and
is near impossible to find)

Zombie
Apps

The App Lifecycle

ZOMBIES

You may see in the diagram a little doodle of a zombie. These are apps that suddenly become popular and gain life again in what appears to be some RANDOM growth (Hence the term zombie – Coming back to life)!

There are reasons for this, however and will keep you going in the long run. Sometimes apps are SEASONAL, so you may see an app hit oblivion through the summer months and then in winter months pick up again. When an app goes Zombie, you want to help it get ALL the sales it can by doing a marketing push or using advanced techniques like you will learn in Chapter 12. Zombies need help to grow and can easily become heavy hitters for quite some time.

A great example is our fireplace app called Intimate Fireplace. Our app goes Zombie during the winter and Christmas months. During that time we like to put marketing dollars behind it because it will just come right out of app oblivion because everyone is looking for a fireplace. It starts gaining a rank again on its own and we can then take that Zombie app and grow it.

Other reasons why an app may go Zombie could be specific NEWS or POLITICAL events! Let's say you have a soccer app, and every 4 years is the world cup, all of a sudden during the world cup year, your app goes zombie!

If you watch the news and prepare yourself, you can help your zombies out so they can gain more downloads and increase your overall app infrastructure.

"Habits can make or break you. List your bad habits down and replace them with good ones! Change will lead to success!"

— Abhinav Gupta

12. STEP 4: APP NAME AND KEYWORDS - ASO

Up until this point you have worked hard on creating an app, however I have not told you to name your app yet. That is because what you NAME your app will either increase or decrease your sales! In this next step we must now go over App Store Optimization techniques to name our app successfully with a higher probability of success rather than just blindly naming our apps. Using keywords and app titles in a smart way and researching what has been working for others will help you to increase your downloads and sales over time rather than those who do not optimize their apps for the app store.

ASO App Store Optimization

App Store Optimization is a very powerful trend taking over the entire app marketplace. Choosing the right combination of keywords, icons, titles and screenshots (KITS) can help your app increase in rank throughout the app store. Gone are the days of just putting an app up and praying it will become a number one hit. With now over 700,000 apps in the Apple App Store, competing against all of them will be a challenge. This is where optimization of your app can help to yield more downloads and results.

I highly recommend using the service from AppCod.es (http://www.appcod.es). They literally let you drill down to the keywords that people are using in the market to obtain higher app store search rankings compared to others who have similar apps.

a. Simply setup an account on AppCod.es for $15/month

b. Add an app name or potential app name you are considering naming your app and start adding some keywords you are considering to use.

c. Now search for apps using the search bar inside of AppCod.es and you should see a listing of apps come up.

d. In the listing you will notice that each app has a total download count per month and an overall download count as well. Look at the apps that have high monthly and overall download counts.

e. Of those apps with higher download counts, take note of the app name and keywords they are using. We want to use a similar name and similar keywords.

For example, I have an app in the app store which I had named Quiz Flashcard Maker. This was before I did any form of ASO. After that I did a major update on my app and decided to start ASO and researched that most people were typing in just the word flashcards. After that I looked at the keywords and titles of similar apps and replaced my own keywords and titles and renamed the app to "Flashcards ." (YES there is a period in the title of the app).

This change helped me to rank much higher compared to other apps and instantly if someone searched for flashcards, out of over 1600 apps, mine was in the top 100 this time. That's a HUGE difference from being at the bottom of the list!

f. Now use your newfound information to name your app and prepare keywords which you will enter when you submit your app to the app store.

TIP: Use similar keywords and titles of the top performing apps and you too will start to see an increase in your app rank and downloads!

KITS KEYWORDS, ICONS, TITLES AND SCREENSHOTS

Along with Keywords and Titles, you will also need to have a VERY HIGH QUALITY Icon and equally high quality Screenshots.

A winning combination of KITS can yield a successful application that gets a lot of downloads and is easily found in the App Store.

I highly recommend outsourcing Icon design and Graphics design to specialized graphic artists who have that eye for graphics and colors.

In fact on fiverr.com I've been able to get many great icon designs for just $5 so it's always a great idea to outsource things like this to others, especially when the cost of such things is relatively low. Simply send over your image screenshots and screen captures from your device or running apps, and the graphic designers can add your promotional text and make those screen shots go from boring to stellar!

So go ahead right now and go and get an icon and screenshots made so that you are ready to upload your app to the various app stores and start selling your first app!

CONGRATULATIONS ON MAKING IT THIS FAR!

WELCOME TO THE WORLD OF APP DEVELOPMENT!

So…Now what?

"Formula to success → When you fall, get back up and try again! NOTE: If you fall again, re-read the formula!"

— Abhinav Gupta

13. TRACKING AND SALES

As you develop your app business, you will be getting a lot of information daily. Sales volumes, application downloads, a number of apps in various markets, total revenue, etc. From this you want to be able to draw various conclusions to help you grow your app business. Let's face it, if you don't know your numbers, you have no idea where you are or where you're going in your business.

You need to know WHAT specific numbers will help you, and you are doing this because with that specific information you can make an educated judgment call on choosing various markets or canceling low performing markets. Numbers will help you determine how to plan your marketing strategy or also how to prepare for upcoming costs.

Knowing your numbers can be very crucial in the App Business so that is why we are going to go over some very special areas to track.

A. FUNDAMENTAL TRACKING

Fundamentals are tracking non-numerical things. Usually this is the market news or latest product announcements. Finding out that a new app market is about to come out or the next tablet device could help you gain more revenues in the future, you can start preparing your apps for that new market. Fundamental tracking is important because it helps PREPARE you for changes in the market. Always keep up to date on the latest fundamental news from top news sites on technology. I personally am subscribed to several major news agencies who are in technology, including Reuters, CNN and even Gizmodo and CNET.

B. TECHNICAL TRACKING

This is the actual tracking of numbers. You want to know sales volume, sales projections, sales revenue, total downloads per market, total downloads per day, what's your best days, what's your worst days, etc. Technical tracking is the real meat and potatoes of your operation and gives you a pulse check of your business. It is done DAILY as well, and you may end up going to the data several times in the day.

To help in your technical tracking, I have created over the past years my special Sales Tracking Sheet! This sheet is available online for download to my readers and for those who are part of my programs, tools and systems.

To obtain this special document as well as the others I have mentioned simply go to the Game Scorpion Website (http://www.gamescorpion. com) and click on the App Trillionaires link. Unlock the page use the following password: **onetrillion**. From there in the downloads list you will see a special spreadsheet document called *salestrackingsheet_ Completed.xlsx*. Simply download and save the file to your hard drive and you should be able to open this document up using Microsoft Excel or even uploading this into Google Docs Spreadsheet and setting it up online. I highly recommend uploading it as a Google Docs Spreadsheet.

TRACKING SHEET BASICS

Before we continue on with using the tracking sheet, please make sure you have downloaded it onto your computer desktop. The following steps assume you have already done this and have the file on your computer.

Step 1. Sheet Setup

1. Upload *salestrackingsheet_Completed.xlsx* file. (NOTE: If it does not look like a Google Docs Spreadsheet, simply inside of Google open the document and click on File → Convert to Google SpreadSheet.)

Concept 1 - UNIT Value = $0.99

Always make sure that every time you enter any sales volume, you enter it in as UNIT VALUE. For example, if you have an app that sells for $1.99, it would be equal to 2 UNITS for every 1 SALE of that app. If you sold 5 apps at $1.99 you would have 10 UNITS that you would enter.

Concept 2 - Daily Inputs

It will be assumed that every day you will be going at 12 AM Eastern Time to check out the daily sales numbers for the DAY BEFORE. For example, if at 12 AM EST your computer clock's date says July 5th, you would be checking SALES for July 3rd. The reason we do this is that sales have not usually finalized until a full 24 hours has passed. Many marketplaces allow time for a user to refund an app and also require time to finalize their numbers.

Alternatively you may also check the numbers early in the morning. The same concept applies, subtract two days from the current date to get the actual day you are going to enter numbers for.

Also if you are on iOS you will notice that sometimes app sales are delayed. This 1 day difference takes into account ALL these factors and for most of the year this 2 day delay works very well. The ONLY time this 2 day delay does not work is during DECEMBER.

Expect to have no sales data being shown to you for many days if not weeks! In fact Apple takes a 1-2 week BREAK during December which means that you can't even SEE your sales volume for at least an entire week during December! Now you know, so BE PREPARED!

Concept 3 - Total Daily Sales

In the sales tracking sheet on the first page there is a long equation. This equation (=B4+B15+B26+B37+B48+B59+B70+B81+B92+B103+B114+B125+B136+B147+B158) will help you in calculating daily sales. It takes into account up to 15 different Marketplaces! As you expand your business you will be able to add various marketplaces which you would like to test into the mix.

Not all marketplaces work well, so later you can always throw a marketplace out of the mix at any time. This equation listed above will calculate the sales for the FIRST Sunday of the month. If I add a SINGLE digit to each Cell number, I will then end up with the total sales for the first MONDAY of the month. For example:

$$=B5+B16+B27+B38+B49+B60+B71+B82+B93+B104+B115+B126+B137+B148+B159$$

Concept 4 - Colored Zones (Green or Aqua)

Throughout the sheets you will notice Green Zones or Aqua Zones. These are EDITABLE areas. Do NOT edit outside of these areas. The sheet will auto calculate everything based on your entries so make sure you only enter in green areas. That being said however, play around with the sheet to try some new things. If you start learning how to work with spreadsheets even more you may even be able to do even more fancy things and get even more interesting numbers spit out to you. For example I was able to adjust the sheet and calculate what percentage of my overall sales each market I had my apps in was generating. These numbers can help you in making decisions in the future to either support a market or totally leave a market completely!

So there you have it, now you can start manipulating the sheet as you wish or learning from my newsletters, programs or other online resources how to keep your sales data up to date and helping you grow your business. Technical and Fundamental analysis of your app business will help you to succeed as the Mobile Industry changes rapidly!

"Dreams are what make life worth living. Dream big! Dream of the BEST! This is what builds hope in life and gives us a reason to try harder!"

— **Abhinav Gupta**

14. APP MARKETING BASICS

*What is **MARKETING?***

Marketing is in a nutshell the process used to inform a certain group (known as a demographic) of certain products or services via various forms and methods (Print ads, Social Media, TV Commercials, Newspapers, etc.) over a certain period of time in order to achieve quantifiable goals (Number of leads, Number of Sales, etc.).

Many people believe that Marketing is ADVERTISING. Marketing is NOT advertising, it is a much more larger area than simply advertising.

A marketing professional requires a lot more than simply an advertising professional, yet many times the two professions are thought to be the same. You can think of advertising professionals as simply those who just create ads in one area and do not really PLAN things out like a marketing professional would. An advertiser is simply a person who just creates an ad and puts it out and keeps repeating the process.

Marketing professionals focus more on a procedure and usually ask the following questions:

1. What are we trying to achieve?

    a. More Sales
    b. More Leads
    c. More Downloads (Not necessarily sales)

2. WHO is our TARGET market?

    a. Focus on ASL (Age, Sex, Location, etc.)

b. Focus on other factors which may help define the market more such as religion, habits, etc.

c. What is the perfect image of your target market? I was once told of a great way to imagine the market for ELECTRONICS → His name is MAT (**M**an **A**fter **T**echnology = MAT).

d. Where does your target market spend most of their time?

e. Keep on trying to define the perfect exact image of your target market

3. What does your target market REACT to?

a. Ex. Men react to sex/sexy ads, also SPORTS ads, also car/technology ads, etc.

b. Ex. Women react to sex/sexy ads of Men, HOME related ads, Jewelery/Shopping ads, etc.

c. Expand on your target market by asking 100 people in your target market what they would like to see in an ad. What people may react to today is not what people reacted to 10 years ago! Even if you think you know your market, doing a market analysis consistently will yield better results.

4. Define what ADVERTISING METHODS you will utilize to attract the specific market to your product/service. Newspaper? Social Media? Print? TV? Radio? Etc. This will be based on a BUDGET that can be spent.

Track results! This will basically be ratios based on amount spent. For example if you show 5000 people an advertisement using various advertising methods and generate 1000 sales, that's a 20% closing ratio (means that you got 20% of the people who saw your ad to make a purchase or to take action). If your app is $0.99 and you paid $1000 for the advertising that's near what we would call a BREAK EVEN point (1000 units at $1 each = $1000). This can help you determine a future marketing push that you can then define after taking in that data and only paying for those marketing methods that had the highest ratios.

Maybe some advertising methods had a 50% ratio vs. others that may have had a 5% ratio. If you keep focusing on those methods that had higher ratios, you'll get better results.

LOCAL MARKETING

When it comes to local marketing of your business the most common attempts from those who are just starting out at physical marketing and advertising methods usually end up being in the print media or non-human interaction areas of advertising. Most people who are new to advertising and marketing their business tend to be afraid of saying hello, and its not that they are afraid of talking to people, it could very well be the main fear that gets most of us and that is the fear of rejection.

Even now after many years of having a solid foundation in Retail Sales as well as learning some of the most advanced method of cold calling and dealing with customers, I still have jitters every now and again about rejection. When you are running a small business, you tend to think sometimes that others will be able to do the job for you, but I can assure you that no one knows your product (in most cases) better than you do, especially if you're an entrepreneur!

So let me cut right to the chase…the BEST most effective way to close any sales deal is WORD OF MOUTH marketing. Basically what this means in a nutshell is that people tend to trust a person over an advertisement. Secondly, they tend to trust a real human being over a salesperson.

So how do you:

a. Meet People who would be interested in your business

b. Not "SELL" them anything and at the same time increase your sales

Wow does that ever sound challenging?

The solution for the first part is LOCAL MARKETING. The solution to the second part is REFERRING BUSINESS to others first and genuinely trying to help the other people make money as well.

Now the stuff I'm about to go over will work for both the App Business and for other businesses as well. Some of the methods I have been using for my app business have been creating flyers, business cards and email lists discussing our latest apps and business. When I meet people I will usually talk less and listen more to them and take a genuine interest in trying to help them out. After meeting them, I generally will follow up with an email and really keep them in mind when I meet people to see if I can find them business. I also ask them if they would like to join up on my mailing list as well and would pass around my newsletter or promotions to those that they feel would be interested as well. This goes into building a solid RELATIONSHIP rather than becoming a sleazy sales person looking to just close the deal. So let me now go over the two areas so you get a solid idea on each.

NETWORKING EVENTS

Here is a list of websites that will help you to find professional business to business and business to customer networking and marketing events in your local areas (Some will charge a cover fee, some will be completely free to attend. ALWAYS dress professional during mornings, semi-professional during evening events and I would not ever recommend to ever go with running shoes and a t-shirt unless there is ever a reason to. First impressions DO MATTER!):

Meetup (http://www.meetup.com): This is the best place in my opinion to find local events in your area. You simply define the search parameters and it shows you all the local physical networking events that are coming up.

Lanyrd (http://www.lanyrd.com): Another great event listing site which lists down many events and even allows you to search them as well. Lanyrd deals more with conferences, however you may end up finding some solid conferences that you can attend and meet many people who may be interested in your apps. If you have built a Health app for example, a great conference would be one with a lot of Health Professionals in it.

Upcoming (http://upcoming.yahoo.com/): This is another conference site, but deals also with many local events that may also be non-business. I'd recommend checking out the conferences and local business networking groups with meetings coming up.

BNI (http://www.bni.com): The grand daddy of networking in my opinion. I learned so very much from joining up to my own local BNI Chapter in the past. If you are serious about networking then BNI is the place to be. The cost may be an issue, but it is well worth it in the long run. If you're looking at networking, or even learning how to become a better networker AND grow your business at the same time, then BNI is the way. The base concept is that 30 or so local business owners get 30-60 seconds to state what it is they do around a table while eating breakfast or lunch. At the end of the meeting, referrals are passed around and deals are made every week!

Eventbrite (http://www.eventbrite.com/): This is a great site to find local business meetings and conferences you can attend.

Eventful (http://www.eventful.com): This is another one of those great event finding websites, however it features events in all topic areas. I highly recommend searching through to see what related events are coming up which have business and networking in mind. With a simple search you can find local networking and business opportunities!

Zvents (http://www.zvents.com/): This one is similar to Eventful and requires a search to find relevant networking opportunities.

OTHER GROUPS TO CHECK OUT (Google search these very VERY important groups): Your local Board of Trade, Chamber of Commerce, Lions Club, Toast Masters, and also do a search for local business networking groups! There are many that are available throughout your local area.

BEFORE ARRIVING TO ANY MEETING/EVENT

Firstly before even deciding to go to an event, have a plan of action. Choose ONLY those events that fit your target market or niche best. Don't just randomly start going to an event just because you think

"EVERYONE" is your target market. Not everyone likes "Chocolate Bars" so don't assume everyone is the "MARKET" for your product. If your apps are educational, choose events and venues with local business owners or conferences dealing with the education market. Don't just end up at a "Top Dogs and Puppies" conference thinking you'll be able to get everyone to buy your app! Dogs and Puppies are a VERY different target market than education! You'd be better off hitting up a conference for new teachers or a universities and colleges conference. Okay so now lets move onto some important points before heading to a meeting and during a meeting:

1. Arrive EARLY by 15 minutes, but don't be there so early that you distract the organizers either. Be punctual but don't be a pest.

2. ALWAYS have business cards and marketing material ready. If you're planning to go to a networking event without these basic required items, then don't bother going.

3. Leave your family/life/personal issues at the DOOR! A POSITIVE mentality is required when you go into these events. If you are planning to go in there looking to make friends who you would hang out with over the weekend, then you're in the wrong place. This is a professional environment, so keep it professional.

4. Don't drink TOO MUCH! Several of these events (Such as boards of trade or chamber of commerce monthly evening networking events) will tend to give you free drinks at the bar. Keep your focus on building relationships, not on just getting carried away drinking. Not only is it dangerous for you, it can make you hurt your business image and could also be potentially dangerous if you plan to drive after that.

5. Don't eat TOO MUCH! Yes you heard me right! Many of these events feature breakfast or lunch. The last thing you want is to be educating a business networking partner on your business only to have to end up going to the bathroom. You never know who you're speaking with sometimes, and the last thing you

want is to walk away from the CEO of a corporation with thousands of employees who may be interested in your apps or to someone who is so well connected that they simply tell people about your apps and your sales increase. I myself one time had to walk away to the bathroom only to find out that the person I was speaking to was one of five owners/partners in a 500 million dollar company with over 2000 employees worldwide!

6. Arrive Early, Stay Late! Networking should never be rushed! Spend time with as many people as you can, and stay late to get to know everyone. There are many times you'll end up spending time with the event creators as well and could lead to a great business relationship that could get you into more venues or even give you the opportunity to speak or present your business in other upcoming meetings.

7. SHOW AND TELL! Always have a reason for your conversations. What are you looking for this week? Did you just develop a new app? Show it! Take your iPad/iPhone along and always have your apps ready to show people. This will definitely get them engaged and will allow you to easily break the ice and start the conversation.

8. LISTEN! Always have a genuine interest in learning about other peoples businesses! Don't just talk and go on and on about your business. This is a sharing experience, and in fact I would recommend talking less and listening more.

9. TALK! Learn to talk at the right times and have a 30 second pitch about your business and how you or your business helps others out. Talk about benefits rather than what you do. Example: "We make apps" does not share benefits of what you do. Something like, "We help people have fun with their iPad/iPhone while bored on a train to work or taking a quick study break at school by creating interesting and fun apps and games" is a better pitch. Another example would be if you are an accountant, you wouldn't want to just say "I'm an accountant", but instead try and show how you help people out, "We help take the stress out

of taxes". You get the point? Make a 30 second pitch on who you are, what's your business, and what you're looking for!

10. DO NOT SELL OR CLOSE A DEAL! The point of networking is NOT to close a deal the first time you meet someone! I know it may seem like a weird statement, but the goal is to build a relationship. You're not in it for the get-rich-quick cash flow, you're in it for the long, consistent, growing cash flow that can only come from a solid business that grows in reputation. Do you want your business to be looked at like it's a "used car salesman" or like a fortune 500 company? The choice is up to you!

BUILDING A RELATIONSHIP

1. After every event, always follow up a day or two later with an email or a call to thank the person and to ask them to join your mailing list.

2. Ask them to go for a coffee to learn more about how you can refer their business better! Book a time to have a professional sit down which will help you to learn more about this person and vice versa.

3. Always respect email rules and never spam anyone. If they do not wish to join a mailing list, don't do it. You're better off forgetting about them and moving onto another potential business relationship.

4. You will ALWAYS find the traveling sales person. Don't get conned into pushy sales people. Also, don't become a pushy sales person yourself.

5. AIM FOR 1-3 months to build the relationship out. During this time, help refer business to people and in turn they will want to do the same.

6. Always thank your referral partners (that's what you call these relationships) for the business they have given to you in the year.

An easy way to do this is to simply send out a thank you card every year. There are many services that can help you out if you have a bulk list of contacts such as one that I have tried before called SendOutCards.com.

"*Challenges happen, you WILL overcome them! Keep positive and believe! Success is right around the corner!*"

— **Abhinav Gupta**

15. MY KILLER APP MARKETING TIPS AND TECHNIQUES

Once you have an active app in the app store and the various app markets, and you've followed all the ASO and KITS advice and have set things up correctly, then the next step involves increasing your downloads and sales volume.

Okay, so now let me share with you some of my killer marketing tips and tricks that I've learned along the way that I know works and can help you increase sales and download volumes!

KILLER TIP #1: LOCALIZED KEYWORDS!

Something neat happens when you start to add languages to your app using what is known as localization...You get another 100 characters for totally different keywords! What I like to do is research keywords in different languages that people would type in and for English based languages I can have up to about 4 different keyword sets! US English, Canadian English, Australian English and British English! This is a really neat tip that has helped me to start gaining higher rankings due to a higher amount of keywords in my apps.

KILLER TIP #2: LOCALIZED TITLES!

You may not be able to get your top coveted title in the US App store, however you may be able to get a translated title that is a hot heavy hitter in another country! This could easily increase your global sales and hence your revenues! Always look for translated titles that can help you increase your downloads!

KILLER TIP #3: HOLD A CONTEST

I have used this successfully time and time again and I end up getting honest feedback and ratings fast, without issues, and all for just giving away a $15 iTunes Gift Card!

a. Simply sign up to TouchArcade.com forums and then post a contest as a developer for a $15 iTunes Gift Card.

b. Purchase your iTunes Gift Cards either from your local Walmart, or from JerryCards.com if you are overseas.

c. Give each valid user review a ticket number and track ticket numbers inside of a spreadsheet.

d. On the draw date you have selected, use Random.org to select a random number from the range of ticket id's you have obtained.

e. Draw a winner and give away the gift card.

Now after the contest you're considered a solid developer as you gain new fans who love you for giving away a $15 iTunes Gift Card. You've also received app reviews FAST! In most cases I usually get a minimum of 10 app reviews and many of them turn out to be pretty decent. The best part is that all of the reviews are HONEST and are helpful in making sure I create the best quality apps. This helps give my app the BEST chance at making it successfully.

KILLER TIP #4: APP UPDATES

Always update your app! Not only will you get more users, you'll also keep your previous users happy!

KILLER TIP #5: PUSH NOTIFICATIONS

I personally can recommend a few push notification services. One that I have used successfully has been PushWoosh.com and another one that I have just started investigating heavily is PushWizard.com.

Push notifications are what I like to call Cash for Clicks! You simply grow your push notification user base over time, then during certain times in the year, change the price of one of your apps that are related to the app that has the push notifications built in and send a push message to that user base.

Instantly you should see an inflow of sales the next day, and in some cases this could mean thousands of dollars from a simple click of the mouse to send your message via push notification. For this reason, I like to call this Cash for Clicks!

KILLER TIP #6: IN PERSON MARKETING

This is one area that not many app developers are doing much if at all! Word of mouth is truly the most powerful method of marketing and what I have done to help increase app sales has been creating flyers and physical marketing material to help me promote my apps in my local market. To add to it, I have created business cards with my website, email, link to the App Store with our apps and my information on it. I then go around to various venues throughout the month and meet with other business owners and individuals to promote my business in person.

On the next pages are a few of the print ready flyers I have made that I use to promote our two apps Intimate Fireplace and My Clock Station Pro.

My Clock Station Pro Flyer
(NON DIE-CUT)

Intimate Fireplace Flyer
(NON DIE-CUT)

KILLER TIP #7: MULTIPLE MARKETS

To make more money and market your apps even more, I highly recommend getting your apps into as many markets as you can. This will help to give you maximum exposure and revenues as you start to grow your business online.

KILLER TIP #8: HARO

This one is an interesting new tool I've been using that has helped me to get my apps out there. It's a website called HelpAReporter.com better known as HARO. On this site, reporters from all around the world come and request pitches for products or expertise from various industries. There are many times where you can easily get your app into prominent magazines and websites simply by pitching your app. This is a great way to really get the word out there! HARO is a secret weapon I've been using successfully for a while now and I plan to continue to use it even more going forward!

KILLER TIP #9: MARKETING FORUMS

There are several marketing forums out there that are always keeping up to date with the latest in Mobile Marketing techniques. The ones I am listing here are ones that I have personally used and am a part of. I try not to spend too much time talking on these websites, but trying to learn and help out others as well, with whatever little knowledge I may have been blessed with in this industry.

Warrior Forum (http://www.warriorforum.com)
Digital Point Forums (http://forums.digitalpoint.com/)

KILLER TIP #10: THE RIGHT PRICE POINT

The sweet spot price now going into 2013 is FREE. Yes you read right… FREE! So how the heck do you make money from something for free? The solution to this is called In App Purchases and Mobile In App Advertising.

This method works extremely well for games, however for utilities and apps in other categories I use a LITE/FULL version method where I release a free version of the app with limited functionality and then using push notifications I hold price promotions randomly.

In the past a common method that also worked well was PRICE FLIPPING in which a person would take their app that was more expensive than $0.99 and would put it down to just $0.99. This also works but not as well as it use to. I find that a better method is to use a Freemium model for games and using in-app purchases let people unlock your app. This same method has been used in the software industry for years and was known as "SHAREWARE" in which a user would get a limited functionality app and would purchase a full license to unlock all the features.

Freemium is now becoming the norm, however I still urge you to try out the various techniques to see what works best for your app. It may be a mixture of several methods or maybe one specific method, but you'll have to keep tweaking and testing until you get it just right!

Each app is a different beast so what works for one app in pricing may not work for another one. In any case always try and monetize your apps using In-App advertising and Push Notifications!

KILLER TIP #11: LOCALIZATION

Localization is a fancy term for simply changing the language of your app from English to another language around the world. By doing this you open up your app to a worldwide audience and an increased chance at sales. You can literally see an increase in downloads simply by having a popular title for your app in a different language or may even start to see downloads from users who finally understand what your app is about.

Another great feature of localizing your app meta data and info is that you can gain another chance at adding even more keywords and screenshots to your app, which in turn means MORE marketing and a higher chance of downloads. In any case, localization is a great way to really push your app to its maximum potential.

Okay so now you know some killer tactics you can use to help grow your business and increase your downloads and revenue. What comes next is having a killer mindset to handle your newfound income!

"*Successful people do what unsuccessful people would consider HARD WORK or BORING AUTONOMOUS work. Only persistence yields results!*"

—Abhinav Gupta

16. THE MILLIONAIRE MINDSET

I personally decided to write this book because I wanted to help people who share the same vision of not only helping themselves and their families, but also giving back to their local communities. I wrote this book to help build RESPONSIBLE wealthy and successful people.

When you grow larger I would love to see you give to those who are less fortunate. If someone has lost a job and is NOT qualified, be charitable if you have the resources and pay for that person's education and HIRE THEM in your business! You would have helped not just one person, but possibly an entire family keep a house and not go bankrupt (like what happened to me). Help out your local communities, schools, hospitals. Be responsible with the money and abundance you have been blessed with!

That is my mission with this book. If you follow what I have outlined here, you should most likely become quite wealthy financially.

In order to really grow this business and keep at it when times get tough, you require a top notch positive mindset. Getting this mindset can be a challenge, but I've laid out some steps you can take right now to help you on the path of creating that abundant mindset that will help you succeed!

So lets start off by asking yourself this important question:

WHY ARE YOU HERE?

Have you figured out WHY you are doing this?

STEP 1 – DEFINE YOUR VISION

If you want to become a millionaire to pay bills, then you're in the "Get Rich Quick" mentality. You'll be focusing on your debt and trust me, that will NOT get you rich at all, not even close!

In fact most people who have become millionaires (and I'm not talking about the lottery wins or those who got it from inheritance) are the ones who had a great VISION! Their vision was SO large that it was all that they could see.

What is your great vision? Where do you see yourself in the next 5 years? 10 years? 50 years? What do you believe your purpose is here?

I truly believe we all have a reason to be here, a powerful purpose, a vision! Maybe one of you could end up curing aids, another person could help out little children, some one else could focus on creating beautiful music that could help heal the soul of millions!

Come up with a powerful vision and let that help MOTIVATE YOU whenever you ask yourself "Why Am I doing this?"

I was there many times as well and asked that same question, but because I had a MASSIVE VISION for my life, I was always able to keep on keeping on!

STEP 2 – DEFINE YOUR THOUGHTS

Thoughts are THINGS! You may have heard this very statement several times in various places. It is very true! What you think about is what you have the potential of creating. Whatever you think about the most is what tends to happen.

You may think this is all nonsense, but it is true. If every day you surround yourself with negative thoughts and negative people, you are going to most likely get negative results.

Change that and start surrounding yourself with positive thoughts and positive people and your results will end up being positive!

Unless you can change your mentality, it will be very hard to hit success AT ALL!

Focusing on what you want rather than what you don't want is the key to watching your thoughts! Go to "HAPPY" places that you know will put a smile on your face and will allow you to change your thoughts to those of "I CAN" and "EVERYTHING IS POSSIBLE".

STEP 3 – INCORPORATE THE FOUR KEYS TO SUCCESS
Faith, Belief, Positive Mindset and Persistence!

These four keys to becoming successful are important, and in my opinion, a requirement to success.

In my life I went through many of these phases where I would have either Belief in myself, but none of the other qualities. Or I would persist only to be miserable (This is the whole "JOB" example, where you are constantly persistently going to work, but you don't like it).

You need to have all FOUR items to truly start seeing success! In order to make your vision of your future real, you need to **BELIEVE** that it is possible. You need to have a **POSITIVE MINDSET** about it. You need to **PERSIST** at making it a reality AND during times of falling down (always remember persistence means you get back up again), having **FAITH** in a higher power (in my case I prayed to God all the time) will be the glue to make everything connect, especially during times when things may seem impossible!

STEP 4 – DEFINE YOUR BUBBLES
So what is holding you back? Usually it's your own self in most cases, and a large contributing factor to this is the concept of BUBBLES! We live in various bubbles, some big, some small, but each bubble is a specific group of people. This could be a bubble of people who all earn 40-50k. It could be a bubble of factory workers, or a bubble of family, etc. We have several bubbles that we are a part of on a daily basis, and this group tends to help mold our thoughts and ways of life.

The reason I have given it the term "bubble" is because until we STEP OUTSIDE of this bubble, we don't realize what is TRULY POSSIBLE!

Take for example a bubble consisting of friends who all make 40k-50k per year and all own a house and have families. Ask any of them to go out for a $100/person dinner, and you'll have them flinch at the price! Take the next bubble of friends who are all DOCTORS, and you will have them not even think twice about the price.

In most cases we are stuck in various bubbles due to our families. These are the more challenging bubbles to be stuck in and it can be quite hard to "look outside" the bubble to see what is possible.

If your bubble consists of people who have NEVER thought of millions or could NEVER imagine themselves even making millions, they will think you are crazy! Ironically the methods they follow do NOT attract millions of dollars, nor do their lifestyles show that they are living like millionaires. So chances are, if you are "NOT" with them and copying them and living in their lifestyle, you are "NOT" the same and they cannot "RELATE" to you. HENCE you cannot build a lasting "RELATIONSHIP" and that's where friendships die off.

You may have heard many people say, "Oh money changed them, they no longer are friends with me". In most cases the irony is that in order to MAKE MONEY you need to change the bubble that you are a part of, and people in your original bubble will NOT understand that. Because you will be more focused on doing things the people in the abundant bubbles do, your original friends from your original bubble will think that you've changed or that "money" changed you. It is actually quite far from the truth, and in actuality you could not have changed until you stepped outside the bubble and looked at what was possible.

Even till today I have many friends/family who just don't understand why I don't have a "JOB". Until I stepped outside of that "bubble" I didn't know that you don't have to have a job, but could actually love what you do and live a life that is EXTRAORDINARY! I now have a Career, I really don't work, I love what I do and enjoy it! This is something that my original "bubble" of friends and family just do not understand. They call it weird and every time I meet these same people from that bubble, they always try and find some way to "RELATE" to me and always try and get me to either get a "JOB" or do things that they can "RELATE" to because they have never stepped outside the bubble and just want you to be a part of their bubble.

I actually had one person get so upset at me because I was "SMILING" about life.

"HOW CAN YOU BE HAPPY? YOU DON'T HAVE A JOB! AREN'T YOU MISERABLE?"

The irony was, they were miserable and I was happy, and that was what got them even more upset, they wanted me to be miserable with them so that they didn't feel that they were crazy and the "only one" who was miserable!

If you can't smile in life, quite frankly you're wasting your time doing the wrong things. And I'm not talking about waiting for the RIGHT TIME to be happy and grateful. You should be able to be happy and grateful about life at MOST times (Obviously I'm not saying go to a funeral and start dancing and laughing, that's not what I mean by this). But for most times in your life, you should be able to really enjoy and smile about it and say, "WOW this is amazing! I can't believe I **GET** to do this!"

As you become an app developer, and start going outside of your bubble, expect to meet many from your original bubble who just don't understand or relate to you. That's because you are stepping outside of your original bubble to see what else is possible, and I can assure you here and now that ANYTHING YOU PUT YOUR MIND TO AND BELIEVE WITH FAITH AND A POSITIVE MENTAL ATTITUDE IS FULLY POSSIBLE!

STEP 5 – VISUALIZATION

Ok so now onto some visualization tools and exercises. So how do you visualize abundance? Lets start at the root of it, which is MONEY.

Here is a great website that provides a tool that you can use to gain the MENTALITY of abundance. It is called UnlimitedUniversalBank.com by Megan Jenifer. You simply put your email address in, and every few days to every week, you get a VIRTUAL DEPOSIT of $1000 into a virtual bank account.

If you treat it like a real bank account that you never can take money out of, you will start to notice that as it accumulates, your EMOTIONS of abundance start to grow. THAT IS THE KEY!

You want to build an emotional feeling of abundance, and soon enough this emotion will allow you to start focusing on the things that WILL gain you even more abundance. Pushing your vision forward, you'll be able to achieve great things using this simple technique.

The second tool is known as a VISION BOARD. A Vision Board simply put is a board that you put ANYTHING you would like to have in your life on. Imagine if there were no limits and no restrictions on time, money or resources. If you could have anything, what would you get? Place this on your Vision Board, and then every day come and take a look at it when you wake up and before you go to sleep. For example you may take the body of a physically "sexy" person that you may want to have a body like and cut out your head and paste it on top.

You may take a photo of the car you want to drive and then take a photo of you and paste it on top in such a way that you are sitting inside the car. The more you can be a part of ALL of these images, the more real it will feel and hence the emotions will grow and you will really start to feel that you HAVE these things.

After doing this exercise daily for years, I was able to obtain things that I simply put inside of my own vision board. Around 2007 I created a vision board, and one of the things on the Vision Board was, "I will only work on my Dreams and Goals and have only myself and God as my boss". Here I am now in 2013 and I am LIVING THAT!

Here I am writing a book and I've already created a Video Game Business and I plan on taking the money I earn to not only help myself and my family but also create a Charity one day giving back to the world.

Because my vision has been so large, whenever I felt like giving up or whenever I felt that I was not going to make it, I looked back at my great vision and said, "I have to make it, there are people who need me, I must keep on moving forward, keep persisting!"

Have a large VISION and use these tools of Abundance and Visualization to help in creating that great vision!

STEP 6 – RECOMMENDED READING

These are the books that I have personally read (Except a few of the holy books) and can HIGHLY recommend. They helped change me (For Better!) and put me in a mind and state of success and abundance and also helped me to see outside of my own bubble.

Over the past 10 years I have amassed a great library which I believe is even more important than money because it helps me get in the mindset to generate abundance and create an abundant lifestyle. (A Small list of the over 100 Books that I have personally read!)

BOOK LIST:
Think and Grow Rich by Napolean Hill

The Richest Man In Babylon by George S. Clason

Success Through a Positive Mental Attitude Napolean Hill and W. Clement Stone

The Power Of Positive Thinking by Norman Vincent Peale

Get The Edge PROGRAM by Anthony (Tony) Robbins

The Science of Getting Rich by Wallace D. Wattles

The Greatest Salesman In The World by Og Mandino

7 Habits of Highly Effective People by Stephen R. Covey

The One Minute Manager by Kenneth Blanchard

Your Holy Book (For whatever your Spiritual Beliefs Are) → Bible, Quran, Torah, Gita, etc.

"Often family and friends give up on YOUR dreams & goals, because they are **YOUR** dreams & goals. Believe in yourself, even when no one else can!"

— *Abhinav Gupta*

17. APP BUSINESS ACCOUNTING BASICS

Are you serious? You really need to know accounting?

YES! For any business, whether it's an App Business or a Clothing Store, you will require accounting to help keep track of sales revenue, expenses, and even paying your own payroll! Most Governments around the world have an internal body that governs the taxes we pay on the income we earn and in turn help local communities, such as your own, to build and grow. Your taxes therefore are the reason why you experience better roads, safer communities, higher education and many other great benefits depending on where in the world you may live.

That being said, there are two MAIN reasons why we want to keep track of our transactions:

To figure out the taxes that we will be required to be paid at the end of the year

1. To see where we are spending our money the most so that we can make future business decisions based on what we see from the numbers.

2. To help secure various services or loans such as bank loans, asset insurance, mortgages on property, etc.

A great statement that is often stated is that, "The numbers don't lie". At the end of the day you can see positive cash flow coming in, however if you don't track your expenses, you may see the money leave as fast as it comes in. You may think you are making money, but if your "BOTTOM LINE" (This is the number calculated after all costs are subtracted from all the income basically) is not positive, you're LOOSING MONEY and you do NOT have a profitable business. Therefore tracking where your company is spending can help determine where you can possibly save money in the future.

Other reasons why we want to learn both accounting and taxation is due to massive savings in your App Business! You could be loosing MASSIVE MONEY just because of not knowing some very basic important tax laws!

TIP: If you are an international developer like myself who is outside the United States of America, then make sure you setup a US EIN number also known as an Employer Identification Number. This will require you to fill out US Taxes yearly, however that will save you a withholding fee of 30% that the IRS will take from your earnings if you do not have an EIN and fill out US Taxes.

For more details on how to obtain an EIN visit

http://www.irs.gov/businesses/small/article/0,,id=98350,00.html/

FINDING AN ACCOUNTANT

It is highly recommended that you go out to a local college or university and take a single crash course on Accounting 101 or Accounting Basics. In it you will learn basic book keeping as well as generating reports. The basic difference is that book keeping is focused just on inputting information (Like receipts and invoices), but accounting focuses on taking that information and generating reports and charts and analyzing that information so that end users such as business owners or various entities can make DECISIONS based on that analysis.

For example, you hire a BOOK KEEPER to help you put all your receipts into your accounting computer software. Your accountant then goes ahead and generates various reports to show you and advises you on various directions the company can take. You as the business owner would then decide on the actual directions to take based on that info.

Do you cut down on office supply spending?

Do you increase in marketing to generate more sales?

Do we have the money to hire another staff member or do we need to start making cuts to staff?

AN ACCOUNTANT can help you determine this by generating reports from your BOOKS.

So learn that distinction well! Too many people believe that a book keeper and accountant are the SAME thing. They are not and they both have a very different purpose. A book keeper will not be able to tell you these things, their main purpose is to enter in receipts and invoices and make sure that that information is up to date.

There is a THIRD type of accountant is a TAX ACCOUNTANT. Once again we end up assuming that any accountant is capable of taxes as well. A regular accountant may only focus on helping a business owner make decisions by showing them reports of their books, but a TAX ACCOUNTANT focuses on tax savings and tax obligations. The Tax accountants role is to help in planning to save on TAXES or to help reduce the taxes paid by educating the business owner on new government programs that may be available or other things that can help in taxation.

In your business you will be dealing with all three levels of Accountants. You may ALSO learn how to do a few of them yourself. For example, you may go to a basic accounting course, obtain a book keeping and accounting software package like Quick Books or Simply Accounting and then enter the books yourself and generate reports yourself using the software. That is also a possibility and would then require you only to focus on finding a good TAX ACCOUNTANT.

Knowing this distinction between the types of accountants can help save you a lot of money and headache by not hiring accountants without understanding their function. Too many times in the past I would hire accountants thinking that they all did the same thing, and ended up paying them money for only 1 part of the job when I thought they "DID IT ALL".

Don't make that mistake on your own, get the RIGHT type of accountant for your needs!

So how do you find them? WORD OF MOUTH! Ask your friends, ask your family, ask local business owners if they know a good accountant. Go to various businesses that you know are succeeding and ask them who their accountant is and if they would be willing to take on a new client.

"Success happens by taking action on the big dreams by putting it into a __calendar__... otherwise it is just a dream and will always remain that way..."

— *Abhinav Gupta*

18. WINNING SCREENSHOTS AND ICONS

To create winning icons and screenshots, you want to start by telling a STORY! Customers love a brand and a story, especially in apps! I've seen apps that are horrible when you download them, but when you see the screenshots, the stories and icons you end up hitting the buy button. That's where we get the term, ***PEOPLE BUY THE SIZZLE***, even if the food tastes bad, it's all about the hype.

Now if you mix your hype with a great product, you'll have even more downloads, but I've seen too many AMAZING APPS go dead and into Oblivion. Some solid apps have been thrown out, not due to them being horrible, but because their screenshots and icons and description were just not good enough, people disregarded the app.

Great icons and screenshots and descriptions all tell a GREAT STORY! They show the EMOTIONS that a user will be able to get out of a product and go over the fun parts of their apps in an EASY way. Rather than discussing "Feature A", "Feature B", etc., great apps discuss a STORY!

Below is a summary of what you want to do when creating icons and screenshots:

1. Winning Icons

   a. Keep it simple and to the point (KISS METHOD)
   b. Follow your THEME (If your screenshots have a certain theme, keep the colors and images similar)
   c. Make it STAND OUT!
   d. Add little things like CALLS TO ACTION inside the icon.

For example a simple banner saying the word "HOT" can increase your sales. It worked for one of our apps and got our downloads to increase. Black text on yellow banners tend to work really well.

e. Detail in icons can go a LONG way!
f. Think about how your icon will look amongst other icons in a search
g. Draw attention to your icons using your target market. Ex. If your app targets children, putting in a sexy woman would probably not attract that audience. If however your target market was males ages 18-35 a sexy woman may just do the trick! If you were targeting a certain demographic, knowing what you are targeting WILL HELP!
h. Know your market so you can target!
i. KNOW YOUR MARKET SO YOU CAN TARGET!
j. Your icon is the FIRST thing a person sees along with your app title, make it COUNT!
k. Try NOT to have text in your app icon if you can avoid it. Text in an app icon just in most cases does not work well.
l. As you grow and gain more apps, start BRANDING! Redo your icons with a BRAND symbol so your apps are RECOGNIZABLE! Your customers will start to follow your branding.

2. Winning Screenshots

Once you have successfully created your app icon, creating corresponding screenshots is very important! Here are the top things you want to do to make winning screenshots!

a. Always draw your screenshot inside of a frame or tablet. This tends to give a better presentation of your app. In some cases depending on app, this may not be the best thing to do, but in most cases drawing your app screenshot inside of a virtual device/photo frame (like a Polaroid picture) in a screenshot usually has a more powerful effect.
b. List single phrases in your app or single lines in your

app for how to use your app or telling a story. DO NOT overpopulate your screenshot with text, that's horrible!

c. Don't overload your screenshot with images either. LESS IS MORE!

d. If you have a game or an app ALWAYS try and use your main stars to promote your app! People like to see characters/people promoting an app and definitely love when a character promotes an app. For example if you have a video game, use the video game characters to help you sell your app!

e. Have a color scheme that matches your icon. Always try and make the icon and screenshots match.

f. 3-4 screenshots are always best!

g. ADVANCED SCREENSHOTS are those that are made up of 3-4 images side by side to create an entire image. People use this technique to draw attention to their app. Its another great trick that can be used to get attention to your app.

h. UNDERPROMISE...Over Deliver! If your screenshots show a basic set of things that your app does and the user downloads it for that and they get even more, they will LOVE YOUR APP!

i. The easiest thing to do is list your main features and emotional touch points. Ask yourself, "What will my app help a user do/feel?" For example a calculator app may help someone overcome their taxes. A feeling of relief when they achieve their math homework or complete a math assignment. You could use this emotion of relief as a simple statement, "Easy and fast, helps take care of even the most challenging math assignments and will make your accountant smile!" Rather than putting, "Has 10 buttons."

j. Make it relevant to your TARGET MARKET! Here are statements for a calculator for various target markets (NOTE: These would be DIFFERENT calculators made based on the target market):

  i.   Children
       "Fun and colorful with large keys for the smallest of fingers!" (Show an image of a child/children)

    ii.   Seniors
              "Large fonts so you wont need your glasses!"
              (Show an image of a senior with glasses)

    iii.   Men
              "Helps take the guesswork out of that next home
              DIY project!"
              (Show a man standing with a tape measure)

    iv.   Women
              "Stylish and sexy buttons with various themes to
              choose from!"
              (Show a stylish woman in professional attire)

    v.   Those late on taxes
              "Get those calculations done right every time and
              make your accountant drool!"
              (Show a person sitting with paperwork on a table
              looking stressed out)

    vi.   High School Students
              "Cool tools built in so you can ace any math
              exam!"
              (Show a teenager with a backpack holding books)

  k. Putting extra thought into your screenshots can help make
      your apps sell better.

3. Winning Descriptions

Great app descriptions are SHORT, spell-checked and highlights key features, differences and a call to action to buy!

Now we know that most users rarely look at descriptions. In fact only the TOP part of the description (usually the first three lines) is read most of the time with the bottom half being skipped on most occasions. Knowing this should help you to put the most relevant info AT THE TOP!

Any awards, reviews, rankings or anything that is a SPECIAL thing about your app should be placed at the very top of all your descriptions.

Has your app been given a 10/10 star review? PUT IT AT THE TOP!

Has your app been featured in New and Noteworthy? PUT IT AT THE TOP WITH THE DATE IT WAS FEATURED!

Has your app gone on sale for a few days? PUT IT AT THE TOP WITH THE PROMO DETAILS!

Users will rarely click on the MORE button to read a description, most users have already decided to make a purchase from the icon and screenshots. In fact the way a user goes through an app is usually as follows:

1. Icon

2. Screenshots

3. USER REVIEWS

4. Description (If they have not been sold already)

That being said, a winning description tends to do little with your actual app and more with what your app has accomplished or achieved. Of course you want to put what your app does inside your description as well, but place that information right after all the noteworthy things.

For example for the calculator app above (which we were talking about) you could put all the full features and functionality right AFTER all the winning details.

The biggest mistake is hiding the points that make your app shine! Too many people leave out new and noteworthy items or app rankings or even app reviews.

REMEMBER → You're goal is to CONVERT the user to a sale, not simply describe something to them. You want your features there, but your focus should be first on how wonderful your app has done and what others have been saying.

Imagine a cereal box at your local store. Have you ever seen a cereal box that lists all the nutrients and all the ingredients as the FACE of the box? NEVER! It's always tucked neatly away on the side as ADDITIONAL information.

On the front of a cereal box you see the AWARDS and RECOGNITION the cereal company has or new things that make the cereal so great.

Always put a call to action whenever you get a chance! Something that makes the user want to hit the buy button ASAP!

We used this technique in Melina's Conquest and that helped increase our sales after the app went into Oblivion:

Now you know the secrets to creating winning app icons, screenshots and descriptions. This methodology will help you increase your sales for sure!

"*It takes just as much energy to think good thoughts as it does to think bad thoughts...so start thinking of the best! You deserve it!*"

— **Abhinav Gupta**

19. BOOKMARKS LIST

Here is a short list of items that I highly recommend you keep in your web browser bookmarks. These are all the items I have gone over in the book thus far plus several additional websites I have found along the way. I'm constantly updating this list on the App Trillionaires special page I have made on my website, which you can access once again using the password **onetrillion** and by visiting http://www.gamescorpion. com. As stated earlier, I'd highly recommend joining the newsletter and you'll even get a chance to get in on future programs, tools and resources that I am constantly creating for mobile app developers!

A.   Google Docs - https://docs.google.com

B.   LUA Programming Docs - http://www.lua.org/pil/index.html

C.   ShiVa Forums - http://www.stonetrip.com/developer/forum/

D.   ShiVa Wiki - http://www.stonetrip.com/developer/wiki/index. php?title=Main_Page

E.   ShiVa Documentation - http://www.stonetrip.com/developer/doc/

F.   CG Textures Royalty Free - http://www.cgtextures.com/index.php

G.   SoundSnap Royalty Free Sounds - http://www.soundsnap.com/

H.   iTunes Connect Developer Page - https://itunesconnect.apple. com/WebObjects/iTunesConnect.woa

I.   Google Play Developer Page - https://play.google.com/apps/publish

J.   Blackberry ISV Portal - https://appworld.blackberry.com/isvportal/

K.   Amazon Developer Portal - http://developer.amazon.com/

L.   Barnes and Noble Developer Portal - https://nookdeveloper.barnesandnoble.com/sign-in.html

M.   Top App Charts - http://www.topappcharts.com/

N.   App Annie - http://www.appannie.com/

O.   Gimp – http://www.gimp.org

P.   Audacity - http://audacity.sourceforge.net/download/windows

Q.   Gmail – http://www.gmail.com

"As you get closer to success, it will seem like the world is working harder to keep you from it...keep at it, you are almost there!"

— Abhinav Gupta

20. FINAL THOUGHTS AND NEXT STEPS

So by now if you've been following my recommended steps that I've outlined, you should be well on your way to a successful app business.

Your next step would be to go and visit my website at http://www. gamescorpion.com and click on the App Trillionaires link. After that use the password **onetrillion** and start off by downloading all the tools and documents there that will help you on your journey as an app developer. SIGN UP to my newsletter and if you can, join one of my monthly programs where you'll even get a chance to see me via my live webinars and online seminars going over the latest tips, techniques and methods of app development and app marketing. I am looking forward to meeting you and getting to know you as you start growing your app business and becoming a part of the mobile app industry!

I wish you a lot of blessings in your new business and truly hope and pray you will become a responsible successful business owner in one of the hottest businesses to get into right now!

After you have made your first app and put it into a market successfully, I highly recommend replicating it and making new apps and also getting into as many markets as you can.

Use several of the killer marketing methods I've discussed to hit the right sweet spot to gain even more money and sales and keep on building your app kingdom!

It most likely won't happen overnight, but I can assure you that if you just stick to it and keep replicating things, keep tweaking and testing various methods of marketing, you will eventually get to a point where this will really make you a very steady income, even while you sleep!

The world of apps is growing exponentially…will you be the next **App Trillionaire?**

"Today is a beautiful day! You are a winner! You will achieve success! Believe in your dreams, they WILL come true as long as you believe!"

— Abhinav Gupta

About The Author

Abhinav Gupta is the Lead Developer and CEO of Game Scorpion Inc. He is an App Developer, App Business Trainer and even a Motivational Speaker in the Mobile and Technology Industry.

Recognized as a professional in the field, he has had his hand in building and successfully publishing over 25+ apps in over 10+ markets including Apple, Google Play, Amazon, Barnes and Noble, Blackberry, HP WebOS, and several others. He has been developing apps and games for several years and has a passion for creating new things. The apps he and his team have created have been downloaded hundreds of thousands of times across the world in various markets.

With over 10 years in the IT Field, Abhinav has focused on training new and existing Mobile App and Video Game Developers on the latest methods of creating and even monetizing Mobile Applications. With his diverse experience in the IT Field, Abhinav has started to pave the way for new and upcoming app developers and helping to grow the businesses of current app and game developers worldwide.

With books, programs and tools specifically created for the Mobile App and Game Business, Abhinav's hand's on experience are well respected in the industry. He currently develops his apps and games using ShiVa 3D, a powerful cross platform game creation tool.

He has written several pieces on the subject of mobile apps and mobile business and has even been seen discussing his apps, courses and training in several prestigious venues.

www.ingramcontent.com/pod-product-compliance
Lightning Source LLC
LaVergne TN
LVHW092007050326
832904LV00017B/315/J

* 9 7 8 1 4 7 5 9 7 0 4 1 8 *